100 Inspiring Rafflesians

1823–2003

100 Inspiring Rafflesians 1823–2003

Tan Guan Heng

World Scientific

NEW JERSEY • LONDON • SINGAPORE • BEIJING • SHANGHAI • HONG KONG • TAIPEI • CHENNAI

Published by

World Scientific Publishing Co. Pte. Ltd.
5 Toh Tuck Link, Singapore 596224
USA office: 27 Warren Street, Suite 401-402, Hackensack, NJ 07601
UK office: 57 Shelton Street, Covent Garden, London WC2H 9HE

Library of Congress Cataloging-in-Publication Data
Tan, Guan Heng.
100 inspiring Rafflesians, 1823–2003 / Tan Guan Heng.
p. cm.
ISBN-13: 978-981-277-946-5 (hardcover : alk. paper)
ISBN-10: 981-277-946-9 (hardcover : alk. paper)
ISBN-13: 978-981-277-891-8 (pbk. : alk. paper)
ISBN-10: 981-277-891-8 (pbk. : alk. paper)
1. Raffles Institution (Singapore)--Alumni and alumnae--Biography. I. Title.
II. Title: One hundred inspiring Rafflesians, 1823–2003.
LG395.S55T36 2008
373.5957--dc22
[B]
2007039762

British Library Cataloguing-in-Publication Data
A catalogue record for this book is available from the British Library.

Printed in Singapore by Mainland Press Pte Ltd

Contents

Foreword	xi
Preface	xiii
Acknowledgements	xv
Abdul Jamil bin Haji Ahmad *Malaysia's Lieutenant-General*	1
Zaibedah Ahmad *First Career Woman Ambassador*	5
V. Ambiavagar *A Thoroughbred Rafflesian*	9
Johnny Ang *A Disabled Artist*	11
Ang Swee Chai *Doctor Defies Death to Save Lives*	13
Edmund William Barker *The 'Cambridge Blue' Minister*	17
Cham Tao Soon *Of Rabbits and Fish Head Curry*	21
Michael Chan Chew Koon *Lord Chan of Oxton*	23
Alan Chan Heng Loon *The Best of Both Worlds*	25
Kit Chan *A Star is Born*	27
Betty Chen *Like Mother Like Daughter*	31
Bertie Cheng *Mr POSB*	33

Chia Boon Leong *Twinkletoes* 35

Claire Chiang *A Woman of Many Parts* 37

Choor Singh *From Charpoy to the Bench* 41

Chua Kim Yeow *Mr Accountant-General* 43

Lionel Cresson *Pioneering Industrialist* 45

Ridzwan bin Haji Dzafir *Of Trade and Diplomacy* 47

Goh Chok Tong *Second Prime Minister* 51

Goh Choo San *World Famous Dancer and Choreographer* 55

Euleen Goh *On Top of the Banking World* 57

Han Fook Kwang *Newspaper Editor* 61

Albert Hong Hin Kay *Of Bricks and Mortar* 65

Yusof Ishak *Singapore's First President* 67

S. Jayakumar *Judicious Deputy Prime Minister* 71

Hijjas Kasturi *The Architect in Nation Building* 75

Khoo Kay Chai *The Student's Principal* 79

Khoo Tee Chuan *From Bukom to Lumut* 83

Kiang Ai Kim *Of Chemistry and Longevity* 85

Kirpa Ram Vij *Chief of Armed Forces* 87

Koh Chai Hong *The Sky's the Limit* 89

Stella Kon *International Playwright* 91

Kwan Sai Kheong *The Westernised Oriental Gentleman* 93

Kwek Siew Jin *Chief of the Navy* 95

Lee Kuan Yew *Founding Father* 97

Lee Siow Mong *The Chinese Mandarin* 101

Lee Suet Fern *Of Mergers and Acquisitions* 103

Leong Cheng Chit *Paper Wizard* 107

Lim Boon Keng *Rags to Riches* 109

Lim Bo Seng *Nationalist and Patriot* 111

Carmee Lim *The Chatek Queen* 115

Lim Chin Beng *Reach for the Sky* 117

Lim Hng Kiang *A Nuts and Bolts Minister* 121

Lim Hsiu Mei *The Girl Who Guides* 125

Lim Kim Choon *Have Wings, Will Fly* 127

Lim Kok Ann *Of Medicine and Chess* 129

Lim Neo Chian *An Extraordinary Soldier* 131

Lim Pin *Descending the Ivory Tower* 135

Lim Soo Hoon *First Woman Permanent Secretary* 139

Lim Yew Hock *From Clerk to Chief Minister* 141

Low Boon Chye *NCAR Astrophysicist* 143

David Marshall *First Chief Minister* 145

Ernest Steven Monteiro *Pioneer in Preventive Medicine* 147

Mohamed Javad Namazie *A Persian in Malacca Street* 149

Noel Evelyn Norris *Veteran Educator* 153

George Oehlers *Mr Speaker* 155

Mae Noleen Oehlers *A True Blue Rafflesian* 157

Mohamed Taib bin Osman *Pioneer of Pantai Valley* 159

Indra Padmanathan *World Bank Specialist* 163

Pang Eng Fong *Enigmatic Academic and Diplomat* 165

Phay Seng Whatt *Guardian of the Civil Service* 167

Judith Prakash *The Lady is a Judge* 169

A. P. Rajah *An Honourable Man* 171

Quah Kim Song *Deadly Striker* 173

S. Rajaratnam *Author of National Pledge* 175

Zainul Abidin Rasheed *Mr Mayor* 177

T. Kanaga Sabapathy *International Art Historian* 181

V. Sadasivan *Television Personality* 185

Rosie Seow *Pioneering Stage Actress* 189

Benjamin Henry Sheares *Father of Obstetrics and Gynaecology* 191

Shi Ming Yi *The Monk Who Came in from the Cold* 193

Siow Lee Chin *World-Renowned Violinist* 195

Soh Ghee Soon *Father of Amateur Football* 197

Robert Solomon *The Methodist Bishop* 201

Song Ong Siang *Queen's Scholar* 203

Su Guaning *A Farewell to Arms* 205

Leaena Tambyah *The Play's the Thing* 207

Tan Cheng Bock *Taking the Nation's Pulse* 209

Tan Cheng Lock *Father of the Malayan Chinese* 213

Tan Eng Liang *Scholar and Olympian* 215

Tan Eng Yoon *Fastest Man Wins* 217

Tan Hwee Hock *Water Polo Gold Medallist* 219

Tan Lian Ann *Chess Prodigy* 223

William Tan Kian Meng *Impacting Lives Beyond the Wheelchair* 227

Margaret Leng Tan *The Toy Piano* 231

Tan Swan Beng *PWD Director-General* 233

Willie Tann Boon Guan *Poker King of Europe* 235

Abdullah Tarmugi *The Speaker Speaks Out* 239

Alice Tay Erh Soon *Law Professor and Human Rights Champion* 241

Tee Tua Ba *Top Cop Held at Gunpoint* 245

Teng Pei Wah *First Woman Olympian* 247

Teo Ah Hong *First Woman Pilot* 249

N. Varaprasad *National Library Chief* 251

Wee Kim Wee *The People's President* 255

Othman Wok *A Witness to End of Empire* 259

Francis Wong Tze Kan *The Consummate Journalist* 261

Jackie Yi-Ru Ying *Pioneer in Bioengineering and Nanotechnology* 263

Emma Yong *Dim Sum Dolly* 265

Diana Young *High Flying Entrepreneur* 267

Yu Chun Yee *Straddling Two Cultures* 271

Photo Credits 273

Foreword

I thank my good friend, Tan Guan Heng, for requesting me to write the foreword to his excellent book. I wish to make three points.

First, I wish to praise the author. Tan Guan Heng and I were classmates at Raffles Institution. We had many common friends and common interests. As a result, we became close friends. Our friendship continued during our undergraduate years at the University of Malaya (in Singapore). Although we were in different faculties, we were comrades in the University Socialist Club. We were very seized with the great political issues of the day. We were young and idealistic and we wanted to build a better, a more just and equal world.

Just after completing his degree, Guan Heng suffered a serious setback. As a result of detached retinas, which was hard to cure in the early 1960s, he lost his sight, first, in one eye, and, subsequently, in both eyes. Guan Heng's friends rallied to him, boosted his courage and morale, encouraged him to learn Braille and to find a way to make a living. Due to the help of supporters, including President S. R. Nathan, Guan Heng ran a bookstore, located in the premises of the National Council of Social Services, for several years. Subsequently, he moved it to Plaza Singapura but unfair competition from the big bookstores there eventually forced Guan Heng to close the store.

In recent years, Guan Heng has tried to make a living as a writer. He has published two novels which were well received. He was looking for an idea for a third book when I proposed that he should try writing a book of non-fiction and suggested the topic: 100 Inspiring Rafflesians.

Second, I wish to praise Raffles Institution, Raffles Girls' Secondary School and Raffles Junior College. Few in Singapore would dispute the fact that the Raffles trinity occupy the apex of Singapore's secondary education system. They occupy the top of the mountain not only because of RI's longevity but because all three institutions are based on merit and have succeeded in recruiting many of the most talented boys and girls of Singapore, especially those from humble families. I have always admired the fact that RI is indifferent to race, colour and social class. What gets you into the school is your ability. Once in the school, you are taught by some of Singapore's best teachers and empowered by the school's heritage, tradition and values. RI, RGS and RJC seek to inculcate in all their students the culture of excellence and the spirit of public service.

Third, RI, RGS and RJC have produced many inspiring Rafflesians, men and women who have distinguished themselves in their careers and in their service to the nation and the world. They include three Heads of State, Yusof Ishak, Benjamin Sheares and Wee Kim Wee; and two Prime Ministers, Lee Kuan Yew and Goh Chok Tong. In picking only 100 out of thousands of inspiring Rafflesians, Guan Heng was faced with an impossible task. I do not envy him. He has bravely chosen his favourite 100 and I respect his choices.

The book has been carefully researched and written in a clear and interesting style. I congratulate the author and hope that the book will be a bestseller.

Tommy Koh
Chairman
National Heritage Board

Preface

The idea of writing *100 Inspiring Rafflesians 1823–2003* was first mooted by my old friend and classmate, Prof Tommy Koh Thong Bee. He urged me to undertake this monumental project.

The book, which spans 180 years, can be used as a resource guide to Singapore's biographical literature. It should also be of interest, not only to Rafflesians, but also to students and researchers of Singapore's social history. The history of the three schools, Raffles Institution, Raffles Girls' School and Raffles Junior College, is inextricably intertwined with Singapore's development from a British colony to an independent nation. RI was founded in 1823, only four years after Singapore was founded.

Rafflesians have a proud tradition of public and community service. They have distinguished themselves in the arts and sciences, in the community, and in the areas of defence, diplomacy, education, finance, health, industry, politics and sports. Pioneers in their own right, they have made significant contributions to Singapore's emergence from a Third World entrêpot to a First World nation. The Rafflesian diaspora has also found its niche in the world.

The 100 profiles are arranged in alphabetical order. I had to cast my net far and wide to encapsulate them, because of the magnitude and historical perspective of the book. Some profiles have been included because they are colourful and unconventional. Several Rafflesians, who ought to be featured in the book, declined to be included.

My grateful thanks go to *The Straits Times* and the National Archives for their assistance in my research. I am grateful to the members of the Advisory Panel for their encouragement and support — its Chairman, Prof Tommy Koh Thong Bee, Prof Tan Ser Kiat, Wong Siew Hoong, Bob Koh Chin Nguang, Deborah Tan, Winston Hodge and Cheng Soon Keong. I also owe a debt of gratitude to Chew Boon Keng,

Dolly Sinha Davenport, Stella Kon and Jenny Soh for their meticulous research; and to Dr Rosemary Khoo for her patient and painstaking editing. My interviewees have also given me some rare insights into their own character and personality. They have also regaled me with interesting, and sometimes intimate, anecdotes about themselves and about other Rafflesians.

Writing *100 Inspiring Rafflesians* has been a great learning and enriching experience for me. I am privileged to be given this rare opportunity to write my *magnum opus,* which has taken me three years. It is my modest literary contribution to my *alma mater* and to Singapore's biographical literature.

Tan Guan Heng

Acknowledgements

My sincere thanks to the many people for assisting and supporting me in various ways while I was writing *100 Inspiring Rafflesians 1823–2003.*

Mohamed Abu Bakar, Jiwat Advani, M. Ambiavagar, Evelyn Ang, Hedwig Anuar, Maurice Baker.

Chan Ee Yin, Mei Wan, Thai Chwee, Chang Meng Teng, Chee Guan Chye, Linda Chen, Chia Kuang, Xing, Chia Poh Watt, Choh Lian Peng, Nora Chong, Toh Sum, Chu Tee Seng, Chau Chap Jee, Koon Hoe, Daljit Singh, Diu Siew Chuan, Ee Boon Kong, Harry Elias, M. Fernendez, Harold Foo.

N. Ganesan, Gan Han Seng, Michael Goh, Cheng Teng, Chor Hiap, Tiak Theng, Heng Swee Khoon, Ho Tong Yen, R. Joethy.

S. Khattar, Ambrose Khaw, John Khoo, Khor Buck Chye, Koh Cheng Eng, Jo Ting, Kay Yew, Nam Seng, Thong Chye, Thong Sam, Kok Yoke Hing, Kuldip Singh, Kwa Boo Sun, Kwong Lai Fun.

Lam Peck Heng, Lau Way Fong, Amy Law, Johnson Lee, Geok Boi, Soo Ann, Suan Hiang, Lian Hock Lian, Lim Ee Koon, Gek Suan, Ho Inn, Hock Ban, Hock Chye, Hock Siew, Kian Seng, Kwang Hiok, Lee Kok, Puay Tiak, Swee Cheong, Stanley Loh, Looi Weng Chew, Low Fook Cheng, Fook Yiu, Lum Choong Wah.

A. Mahadeva, Ahmat Mattar, T. P. B. Menon, Zarinah Mohamed, Mok Chek Koon, Abbas Nakhoda, Manijeh Namazie, Lily Ng, Choon Hwee, Foong Yin, Yong Hwa, Khaizer Nomanbhoy, Ong Bock Chuan, Guan Bee.

Phang Chee Kiong, Phua Kok Tee, Gopinath Pillai, Poh Siew Aing, Soo Kai, David Pung, S. Rajendran, G. Raman, Seah Poh Chye, David See, R. P. Sharma, Connie Sheares, Sharon Siddique, Sim Wee Kiat, Ivy Soh, Ghiaw Kheng, Siak Hiong, N. Subramaniam, Peter Szeto.

Tai Kuan Teck, Tan Boon Sai, Cheng Lim, Hui Boon, Jing Quee, Joo Kheng, Seng Huat, Siew Lian, Wen Wai, Dennis Tay, Shaw Ming, Soo Tee, John Teh, Teo Chin Chye, Toh Chye Heng, Thung Syn Neo.

S. Vasoo, Voo Sun Lock, Wang Choong Wah, Wee Kiat Lang, Yeow Chin, Yeong Yoon Ying, Yo Kim Wah, Wan Hussein Zoohri.

Tan Guan Heng

Malaysia's Lieutenant-General

Abdul Jamil bin Haji Ahmad

Abdul Jamil bin Haji Ahmad was the first Rafflesian to receive his training at the Royal Military College at Sandhurst. He retired with the exalted rank of Lieutenant-General and was the person directly responsible for the national security of Peninsular Malaysia. He was also the first Malaysian Commandant of the Royal Military College. In his 32 years of distinguished service, he soldiered through the Malayan Emergency, with the UN in the Congo and also during the Indonesian Confrontation.

Jamil Ahmad was born in Singapore in 1929. His primary education at Tanglin Tinggi Malay School and Monk's Hill Primary School was interrupted by the Japanese Occupation. He then studied at Raffles Institution (1947–1950) where he excelled in sports and was a cadet. Raffles had 800 students then, of whom 22 were Malays. Jamil wanted to be a teacher and to serve in the Singapore Volunteer Reserves. As he was the eldest of 11 children and could not afford to go to university, he enrolled at the Teachers' Training College instead.

Jamil was introduced to the Malayan army by a friend, after overcoming parental objections. After his initial training at Port Dickson, he was sent to under-cadetship at Eaton Hall and the Royal Military College, Sandhurst. Among his contemporaries were King Hussein of Jordan and a Nigerian who later became the President of his country. "In those days, the British gentry sent their offspring to join regiments of their Empire. Some country squires even bought their commission. It was not for the money that they joined. It was for status, position and prestige. They joined to enjoy life and for adventure. There were formal dinner nights. It was all great fun and very British. Some of these traits rubbed off on us and I try to maintain the good and adaptable ones." Jamil was commissioned in 1955 as a 2nd Lieutenant. His rise through the ranks was meteoric because of his brilliant record, and he retired as the Lieutenant-General in 1984. His achievements, which include the Command of the Royal Military College and the establishment of the 3rd Division of the Royal Malay Regiment in Malacca, were impressive. His crowning glory came in 1977, when he was directly responsible for the overall security operations for Peninsular Malaysia.

Jamil recalls the Malayan Emergency. "When the Malayan Communist party first struck in Johore and Perak, they were not coordinated. The security forces could deal with them. The Special Branch had good intelligence, while the RAF bombed effectively. The terrorists operated only in small numbers. In one ambush, we wounded and captured a woman." In 1960, Jamil led a Malayan battalion to serve under the banner of the United Nations in the Congo. Its task was to protect the UN Headquarters and to keep the streets clear. He had a narrow escape when the window of his plane suddenly opened, but fortunately, he was pulled back by his colleague. He commanded 1 RMR during the Indonesian Confrontation and was deployed in Sabah. During an air reconnaissance, his helicopter crashed at Pegagau, but it was not due to enemy fire. They were searching for suspected Indonesian paratroopers. He says, "It is said that when one is breathing one's last breath, the memories of one's lifetime flash through one's head. Thoughts of my wife and my daughter flashed through my mind then. My colleague died in the crash. I could not sit up and lie on my back for long, during which time I walked sideways like a crab. Thereafter, I was known as 'The Long-Life General'."

Jamil Ahmad earned several honourable epithets in his career, including 'the buzzer', 'the human dynamo', 'perfectionist' and 'disciplinarian'. He was nicknamed 'the buzzer' because he was always buzzing his men for something or other. He was constantly on the move, a pace others found difficulty to keep up with. A painstaking workaholic, he had a penchant for details. His usual air of urgency could often be mistaken for impatience. When asking his secretary for a file, he would comment, "By the time you get it, the battle would have been fought and probably lost." He was known to be someone who did not mince his words, but his humane side also came out strongly. He knew the first names of his officers and men, as well as those of their wives and children. He was respected as a person who was not afraid of saying what he believed was right. The welfare of his troops was always of prime concern to him.

Jamil Ahmad is highly respected for his intelligence and straightforward ways. A simple but authoritative man, he embodied the essential traits of a good leader.

First Career Woman Ambassador

Zaibedah Ahmad

Zaibedah Ahmad has the unique distinction of being the first woman Ambassador in the Malaysian Foreign Service. Her diplomatic career coincided with the gradual shift in Malaysian foreign policy away from her traditional ties with Britain and the Commonwealth. She also witnessed the beginnings of the collapse of the Soviet-styled client states of Eastern Europe. She diligently applied herself to her tasks with distinction, winning new friends for Malaysia with her intellect, beauty and charm.

Zaibedah studied at Raffles Girls' School (1946–1956) and Raffles Institution (1957–1958). She is an Arts graduate of the University of Malaya. Her father was a Chief Inspector in the Police Force who later became the Coroner of Singapore. Of her schooldays, she recalls, "I was in the same class with my older sister, Norkiah. Her schooling had been delayed by the Japanese Occupation. We were amongst the first and the only three Malay girls to obtain a Grade 1 Certificate in the 1956 Cambridge Examinations. I liked to study in peace and quiet while she liked the music on." Norkiah worked as a Senior Passenger Relations Officer with the Malaysia Airlines System. Norkiah's Rafflesian husband, Sahari Sulaiman, was an outstanding scholar and sportsman. Their younger brothers kept up the Raffles tradition. Abdul Malek became Malaysia's President of the Court of Appeal and a Federal Court Judge. Zakaria, who was inspired by his brother and sisters to get into RI, became Dean of the Faculty of Social Sciences and Professor of Strategic Studies at the National University of Malaysia.

After her graduation in 1963, Zaibedah was attached to Radio Malaya, then Dewan Bahasa dan Pustaka, and later the Research Division of the Prime Minister's Department. As an officer of the Malaysian Ministry of Foreign Affairs, she was posted to the United Kingdom and New Zealand. In 1983, she was appointed Malaysia's Ambassador to Yugoslavia. She recalls being thrown into the deep end of international diplomacy and breaking into an exclusive male preserve. "It was my first overseas posting as Ambassador. Yugoslavia was an unexpected choice, given that it remained firmly socialist. To send a female Ambassador to what seemingly would be a harsh environment, would prove challenging." However, she proved equal to the task. At a state banquet, being the youngest and the only female Ambassador to Yugoslavia, she was accorded the rare privilege to sit at the same table with all eight members of the Yugoslav Collective Presidency. "It was a great honour, not only to me, but to Malaysia."

From 1983 to 1988, Zaibedah was Ambassador to Romania as well, "Romania was an experience in itself. Solidly behind the Iron Curtain, it was the embodiment of Big Brother as described in George Orwell's *1984*. Some Ambassadors had to wait several months to present their credentials to the President. When relating my story to other Ambassadors, I discovered that my experience was far less frightening or sinister than what the others had to bear. I was later told that I was one of the few who waited less than two weeks to see Ceaucescu. Obviously and strangely, he must have liked Malaysia."

As Malaysia's Ambassador to Spain (1988–1991), Zaibedah was responsible for forging closer ties between the two countries. She played a crucial role, at a time when Malaysia regarded Spain as the gateway into the European Economic Community, with its huge market and collective political influence. In 1991, she created history when she became the first ever woman Ambassador to be accredited to Turkey. She was also the first woman to chair the Committee for Commercial and Economic Co-operation of the Organisation of the Islamic Conference, with its headquarters in Istanbul, Turkey.

She retired in 1996 after 30 years of distinguished diplomatic service. A pioneering woman Ambassador, she is a trailblazer and a role model. In the Big Brother environment of Bucharest, she was privately nicknamed 'Malaysia's Mata Hari' by her male counterparts, because of her impeccable credentials, intellect, beauty and charm. Zaibedah Ahmad comes from a family of distinguished Rafflesians. It is indeed rare to find four members of the same family having made significant contributions to the nation in their different professions — diplomacy, aviation, the judiciary and academia. They are outstanding examples of the Rafflesian diaspora who have found fame abroad.

A Thoroughbred Rafflesian

V. Ambiavagar

Velauthar Ambiavagar was a student, teacher and Principal of Raffles Institution. He was the school's 16th Principal and the first Singaporean to hold this exalted office — the only superscale post in the teaching service.

He was born in Jaffna, Sri Lanka, formerly known as Ceylon, the only child of his widowed mother who died early. His stepbrother became his tyrannical guardian. When he was eleven, he was brought to Malaya and admitted into the Methodist Boys' School in Kuala Lumpur. Having practically no English education, he was unable to cope with his studies. His brother coached him, interspersed with kicks and beatings. Then, his teachers gave him lessons after school. Until he was seventeen, Ambiavagar had no focus in life. His failure in the Junior Cambridge Examinations spurred him to study harder.

He was admitted into RI and his perseverance was rewarded with a teacher-training course. When he graduated from Raffles College in 1932, he had expected to be posted to RI. The expatriate Principal told him that there was no vacancy. Hiding his disappointment, he was about to leave the office when the Principal stopped him, "Hey, not so fast, young man. How are you at extra-curricular activities?" Ambiavagar told him that he had captained the Raffles College cricket team and also represented the Ceylon Sports Club at football, hockey and cricket. He then asked that if he were to take charge of all the games and other activities, what would the other teachers be doing. The Principal smiled. "I like your spirit, young man." He got the job.

"RI in 1932 was noticeably different than in 1924 when I was a student. The atmosphere was charged with a sense of purpose and direction. In mental calibre, my Asian colleagues were on par with the expatriate graduates."

Ambiavagar taught in RI for 27 years. He fought against the racial discrimination of colonial rule. There were separate common rooms for Asian and expatriate staff. He coached the school's hockey team and led them to many victories. In his illustrious career, he had taught many students who later became famous in public life. "I have won their success in my heart, like a gold medal set in precious stones."

Ambiavagar retired in 1961, when he was Acting Director and Permanent Secretary of Education. Reflecting on how he had risen to the top of the service, he modestly wrote in his memoirs. "Reputation is a mere bubble that bursts and disappears. The substance for me was the immediate pleasure in seeing the faces of my pupils glowing with happiness at their success in their studies and in other activities, with my help. World War II, the Japanese Occupation and the loss of many qualified teachers had propelled me to an unexpected dizzy height. Although I favoured my contribution to the cause of education in Singapore, I missed the happy faces of pupils and the appreciative smiles of teachers. I would have preferred life as Principal of RI."

His three children, Mahendran, Indra and Rajendran, hail from Raffles and are all doctors. Indra remembers her father with these words, "My father was a warm, humorous family man who placed great value on family life. His passion was sports and reading. He excelled in hockey, cricket and tennis and later golf. His dedication to sports contributed largely to his longevity of 95 years. In reading, he loved the classics from Shakespeare and Chaucer to Yeats."

A Disabled Artist

Johnny Ang

Johnny Ang is the first Singaporean to receive the International Victory Award, which recognises physically and mentally disabled people who show courage and strength, and are role models for others. He is also a journalist and mouth artist.

He studied in Beatty Secondary School before joining the RI pre-university Science class, where he was a promising student.

A diving accident in Johore damaged his spinal cord and paralysed him from the neck downwards, changing his life forever. "Anyone who has gone through the ordeal and says he has never thought of killing himself is lying. For about seven years after the accident, I was an emotional wreck. I had no self-esteem and no self-confidence. I was ashamed. I refused to meet anyone. The self-pity was overwhelming. On bad days, I even growled at the nurses."

Winning an international essay competition in 1968 started him on the road to recovery. While in Hong Kong to receive the prize, he was forced to make a speech. It was then that he realised that he could overcome his self-consciousness and contribute to the cause of the disabled. Years later, he asked his friend to bring him back to the scene of his fatal accident at Johore's Lido beach. He sat silently for a long while. He felt no regrets, anger or pity. He had passed the test.

At Mount Alvernia Hospital, where he has been a patient since 1961, Johnny Ang is a household name. Singaporeans read about him and visit him, marvelling at his courage and indomitable spirit. He always inspires them with his eloquence and zest for life. Johnny

Ang has received many accolades and awards. "I'm grateful for this recognition. People should realise that a disabled person is not just a label, but a person."

He is the Editor of the *Handicapped Digest* which is published by the Handicapped Welfare Association. He visits the interviewees in their homes with the aid of volunteers. He became a mouth artist when a disabled artist told him that he had the talent and threatened to break off their friendship, if Johnny did not take up the challenge. The constant pain in his neck sometimes causes him to lose control of the brush. His limited movements only allow him to cover 15 square centimetres of canvas each time. He paints mainly in acrylic and oil, and averages eight works yearly. He derives an income from his writing and the sale of his paintings.

Johnny Ang describes himself as 'a pragmatic opportunist' who is not afraid to ask for assistance from his many friends and well-wishers. But he insists that he is not a role model. "Actually, I'm a less than ordinary person trying my best to live an ordinary life in extraordinary circumstances."

Doctor Defies Death to Save Lives

Ang Swee Chai

Ang Swee Chai is an orthopaedic surgeon who risked her own life to save the lives of others. Her courage and self-sacrifice in the Palestinian refugee camps of Sabra and Shatila in the 1980s are legendary.

Ang was educated at the Kwong Avenue Primary School and Raffles Girls' School in the 1960s. She graduated in Medicine from the University of Singapore in 1973. Her parents were in the anti-Japan Resistance movement, and were imprisoned and tortured during the Japanese Occupation. Their sacrifices were an inspiration to Ang. She represented RGS at chess, and was keen on music and reading. She attributes her unconventional lifestyle to her schooldays. "We had dedicated teachers who taught us to think for ourselves and be independent. I also learned that Science, to be meaningful, must be channelled to alleviating suffering and poverty. So, I chose to study Medicine."

Ang Swee Chai is only one of the 16 female orthopaedic consultants out of 1,800 in Britain. She is attached to the prestigious St Bartholomew's Hospital in London. She spearheaded a multimillion dollar charity for displaced Palestinians. Her commitment to their cause is outlined in her inspiring book *From Beirut To Jerusalem*. "In 1982, I walked out of my job in a London hospital and left for Beirut. The Israeli army had invaded Lebanon. Its declared target was the PLO. I was shocked by the daily news reports of the bombing of Beirut and felt called to help the wounded. Within a few weeks, I found myself in the Palestinian refugee camps of Sabra and Shatila."

Sabra and Shatila were more like shanty towns, densely populated with buildings, markets and schools. She was plunged into the *Intifadah* or uprising, the Campaign of Civil Disobedience by the Palestinians against Israeli Occupation. The Christian militia replied with lethal force using plastic-coated metal bullets, tear gas and grenades, even when children were throwing stones at them. "On the morning of 16 September 1982, the casualties started flooding in. Women, children, old people. They had been shot at close range with machine guns. By evening, I found that gunmen were shooting whole families in their homes. More than 2,000 people took refuge in the hospital. I had to operate non-stop." As the drama unfolded, thousands were slaughtered. Two days later, Ang was forced at machine gunpoint out of the camp and into the streets. She passed groups of people surrounded by soldiers, looking desperate and frightened. "A woman tried to give me her three-month-old baby boy. I held him for a few seconds, but a soldier placed a gun against her head and forced her to take the baby back. The soldiers pushed us on with the butt of their machine guns and we marched on. They put us through a mock execution. But, all I could think of was that Palestinians and their Lebanese neighbours were being killed back in the camp. I was so angry that I never thought that my own life was actually in danger."

In 2002, Ang revisited the mass grave where 1,200 were buried during the Sabra and Shatila massacre. "Personally, I have agonised over the situation for 20 years. But, now I have come to the conclusion that it is not a question of vengeance and retribution. It is a question of how the next generation of Palestinians and Lebanese can live in dignity and peace and security."

Ang Swee Chai, the pint-size orthopaedic surgeon, launched her crusade for the Palestinian cause at the age of 34 when she first stepped on Lebanese soil in 1982. She founded and spearheaded the Charity for Displaced Palestinians. In 1987, for her relentless work and courage, she was awarded 'The Star of Palestine', the highest award for service to the Palestinian people, by Yasser Arafat. In the same year, she was voted one of the 'Ten Most Admired Women in the United Kingdom'.

For almost two decades, her heroic exploits, always at the risk of her own life and limb, have been exemplary and inspiring. Her husband had often jokingly told her that she would probably be brought home in a body bag. Her gentle demeanour belies her unflinching commitment and compassion for the oppressed. Beneath this veneer of vulnerability is a very courageous and fearless woman who lives up to her ideals.

The 'Cambridge Blue' Minister

Edmund William Barker

When he was a schoolboy, Edmund William Barker read how the British Empire was won on the playing fields of Eton. His sporting feats in Raffles Institution, Raffles College and Cambridge were later equalled by his political achievements in a newly independent Singapore. He was highly regarded as a lawyer and government minister, and known for his sense of humour. As a sportsman and a politician, he always played the game.

Born in 1920, Edmund William Barker was educated at Serangoon English School and Raffles Institution, where he was the school captain, Head Prefect and champion athlete in 1938. He represented Raffles College in cricket, football, rugby and hockey. He was also the College's champion athlete in 1940. After the Japanese Occupation, he was awarded a Queen's Scholarship in 1948 to study Law at Cambridge. While concentrating on his studies, his passion was still in sports and he was the Varsity's Badminton champion, thus earning a Cambridge 'blue'. He also represented Singapore at hockey. A brilliant sportsman, the only game he did not take up was golf. He loved horses and was a familiar figure at the Singapore Turf Club.

Barker practised Law from 1952–1964. His political career began in 1963 after he won in the Tanglin Constituency on a People's Action Party ticket during the Singapore General Election. His success was repeated in 1968 and 1972. He was Speaker of the Singapore Legislative Assembly and was appointed the Minister for Law in 1964. During his 24 years as Law Minister, he also held the National Development, Home Affairs, Environment, Science and Technology, and Labour portfolios.

Barker's legal expertise was invaluable and very much in evidence when he single-handedly drafted the Separation Agreement between Malaysia and Singapore in 1965.

A distinguished Eurasian leader, Barker forged closer ties and rapport between the Eurasian community and the other communities. In the true spirit of multiracialism, he worked hard to improve the lives of Eurasians, but never at the expense of the other communities.

To his friends and to those in sporting circles, he was affectionately known simply as 'Eddy'. Sports was in Eddy Barker's blood, as an athlete and administrator. As the President of the National Olympics Council, his sports legacy will always be remembered by present and future sportsmen and women. He was the inspiration behind the building of the National Stadium. Singapore had not been able to host the South East Asian Games until 1973, due to the lack of facilities. He was also responsible for the creation of the Toa Payoh Swimming Complex and Games Village. In addition to sports, he also loved music. At parties, he would play the guitar and sing for his friends. His friendliness and humanity made him much loved by the people of Singapore.

Othman Wok has fond memories of Edmund William Barker. "The first time I saw Eddy Barker was in 1938, when I joined RI. He was the Head Prefect, always immaculately dressed in full suit complete with a necktie. My friends told me that he was a 'powerful chap' and that he could send any student to detention class for the slightest mistake or misbehaviour. While walking round the school, he always looked serious and I never saw him smile. One morning, he reprimanded me for coming to school late. I had overslept. On another occasion, he caught me eating *mee goreng* in class during recess and sent me to detention class.

"In 1942, Singapore was ruled by the Japanese military government. I met Eddy again at the Japanese military establishment, the OKA 9420 Butai, situated in the vicinity of the Singapore General Hospital. I was working as a laboratory assistant in the Anti-Plague Department then. He remembered me and looked cheerful. He had joined the Anti-Malarial Unit and was going to Thailand to work at the Death Railway.

"Eddy was a natural sportsman and he represented Raffles at hockey, cricket and tennis. Because of his interests in sports, I proposed

Eddy as the Chairman of the Singapore National Olympic Committee, an appointment he held for many years. A good musician, he played the trumpet in the Raffles Cadet Band and he also played the guitar very well. Sometimes, he played it at functions organised by former Members of Parliament. As a Cabinet colleague, he was a good minister and got on well with all his colleagues, particularly with Lee Kuan Yew, and with his sense of humour, he often created laughter during Cabinet meetings. Eddy and I got on very well, as his friendly attitude and humour brought us closer together. Eddy was also very close to his family and they were always very happy."

Barker was a devoted husband and father. His daughters, Carla and Deborah, have followed in the footsteps of their illustrious father into the legal profession.

Of Rabbits and Fish Head Curry

Cham Tao Soon

Cham Tao Soon wanted to be a musician. However, his father discouraged him and he graduated with a degree in Engineering. He became an academic and subsequently, the founding President of Nanyang Technological University. He was responsible for transforming NTU from a small engineering institute into a premier university in Asia. As a person, Cham does not confine himself only to the nuts and bolts of his profession but also has a passion for the arts, rabbits and fish head curry.

During his early years, Cham attended a Chinese school and Pasir Panjang Primary School, and later received his secondary education in Raffles Institution. He graduated in Engineering from the University of Malaya and obtained his PhD from Cambridge. He was Dean of the Engineering Faculty of the National University of Singapore.

In 1982, Cham was appointed the Founding President of the Nanyang Technological University. It was the opportunity of a lifetime. But he had no illusions about the daunting task ahead of him. Would NTU end up as the poor cousin of NUS and would employers readily accept its degrees? His fears were unfounded. Using MIT as its model, he made NTU achieve international recognition as a premier tertiary educational institution. Under his dynamic leadership, NTU adopted a more flexible degree structure to give its undergraduates a broader education and outlook. "Any reputable university cannot afford to stay static. They must adapt and change with the times, if they want to do well. I'm not for learning in an ivory tower. We are in the business of training manpower for the economy of the nation."

In his 22 years as its President, Cham brought new dynamism and direction to NTU. He introduced the policy of recruiting staff with industrial experience in addition to their academic qualifications. He also introduced new courses, such as Accountancy, Communications and Life Sciences. Another novelty was his weekly lunch meetings with his deans, which were not held in an air-conditioned boardroom, but in a HDB coffee shop in Jurong. The topics varied, but the food menu was always the same — at the table was always fish head curry, his favourite dish. "NTU is like a third child to me as I have been involved with it since its founding. I'm very attached to it. It's more than just a job."

Music is an integral part of his life. He recalls that his childhood ambition to be a musician was wisely vetoed by his father. He possesses 1,500 CDs, including 70 versions of Rachmaninov's *Piano Concerto No. 3*. He plays several musical instruments, such as the piano, oboe, violin and the recorder. He regrets throwing away his old records, which are now collector's items. As Chairman of the Singapore Symphony Orchestra, he wanted SSO to shed its image of catering mainly to an English-educated elite and to raise it to the level of a national orchestra reaching out to a wider audience.

Born in the Year of the Rabbit, it is not surprising that Cham keeps a menagerie of rabbit figurines and has 60 ties with rabbit motifs. Perhaps he can best be described as a romantic, especially when his favourite author is Somerset Maugham. He is a rare combination of the scientist and the artist. In RI, Cham excelled in the long jump and high jump. He also represented the Singapore Combined Schools in table tennis. Nowadays, he is content with exercising every night on a stationary bike or rowing machine.

When Cham Tao Soon retired as President of the Nanyang Technological University in 2004, he was conferred the title of Professor-at-Large, and as Chairman of the Nanyang Academy of Fine Arts, his love for the arts has come full circle. More recently, he has been appointed as the Chairman of the Singapore Institute of Management, with the mandate to turn it into Singapore's fourth university.

He says, "I was privileged to study at RI, the premier school. I had friends from all walks of life and different ethnic groups, and I have greatly benefitted from this."

Lord Chan of Oxton

Michael Chan Chew Koon

Michael Chan Chew Koon alias Lord Chan of Oxton read Dick Whittington, and how the streets of London were paved with gold as a schoolboy and a British subject. As Lord Chan of Oxton, he journeyed there to debate with the British nobility and aristocracy. He was the first Singaporean and the first Chinese to be appointed as an independent life peer in the House of Lords. His father, Chan Chieu Kim, was a former Principal of RI and the first Commissioner for Civil Defence.

Michael was born in 1940 and educated at Serangoon English School, and later at Raffles Institution from 1952 to 1957. He was a Boy Scout, and was also on the editorial board of *The Rafflesian*. "I have fond memories of our friends and teachers. Freedom to experiment within the science labs was much appreciated. Botany was learned by visits to the Botanical Gardens. I enjoyed camping. At RI, we were taught by expatriate teachers. This was helpful for me when I went to study in a British university. I treasure photographs of the old RI. We were very near to the Odeon and Capitol cinemas, useful places of entertainment and milkshakes. Also places to impress the girls in Form 6."

Chan graduated from his medical studies at Guys Hospital in 1964. His postgraduate qualifications, which included an MD from the University of Singapore and MRACP, FRACP, FRCP and a degree from the Royal College of Paediatrics and Child Health, were impressive. He was also the author of several books on neonatology and paediatrics. He was appointed senior lecturer and consultant paediatrician in 1973 and awarded a visiting fellowship at the Institute of Child Health in the University of London.

In 1976, Chan was offered a six-year contract by the Liverpool School of Tropical Medicine, as a senior lecturer and consultant paediatrician. During this time, he taught postgraduate doctors from all over the world and lectured in Libya, Sweden and Germany. He also researched on neonatal jaundice and tetanus in Nigeria and led health teams caring for mothers and babies to five Indian states.

The year 1994 marked a change in his professional career when he was appointed the Director of the National Health Service Ethnic Health Unit. His interests in this area had developed after the riots in Liverpool in 1981 and his work with the Commission for Racial Equality, which champions the victims of racial discrimination in Britain. As the Director, he pioneered the monitoring of patients on a voluntary basis in hospitals. In 1996, the University of Liverpool appointed him Honorary Professor of Ethnic Health. He studied hypertension in Black Americans in New Orleans. In 2000, he decided to take early retirement from the National Health Service.

In 2001, Chan was conferred life peerage in the House of Lords — one of 13 non-partisan peers appointed from 3,000 applicants. As Lord Chan of Oxton, he held the honour of being the first Singaporean as well as the first Chinese to be conferred this prestigious title. Issues on health, children, ethnic minorities, tropical diseases, human rights and racial equality were his special interests. He relished the privilege of being in the heart of government and getting to air his views nationally once a week at parliamentary sittings.

Michael Chan Chew Koon is another shining example of the Rafflesian diaspora who had distinguished himself in the United Kingdom. He died in January 2006 due to an illness. His premature passing was mourned by his many friends and admirers, both in Singapore and in the UK.

The Best of Both Worlds

Alan Chan Heng Loon

Alan Chan Heng Loon has risen to the top of his career in both the public and private sectors. A former Permanent Secretary in the Singapore Administrative Service, he is currently the Chief Executive Officer of Singapore Press Holdings. He was an outstanding student leader and a President's Scholar.

Chan attended Haig Boys' Primary School and Raffles Institution from 1966 to 1969. He joined the National Junior College, where he was a student councillor and school swimmer. "We were among the last batch of students to have studied in the Bras Basah campus. For a boy staying in the far-off suburbs, it was a treat to come down daily and to run off to the Capitol, Odeon and Cathay cinemas every Saturday after extra-curricular activities were over. Compared to the modern amenities of today, the rickety staircases and dark classrooms with a single light bulb was no deterrent to study in the premier institution of Singapore. During Job Week and other fund-raising projects, our Scout troop could usually earn $35,000 annually. We toyed with the idea of acquiring a bungalow for our Scout den, but were refused permission by the school."

Unlike most President's Scholars, Chan did not take the conventional route to Oxbridge. Instead, he graduated in Engineering from the École Nationale l'Aviation Civile. "In the early 70s, scholarships were few and far between. I was only offered one in France and I had no other choice. This was the first time that France was offering the scholarship and I wanted to be in the pioneering batch. Also France was very advanced with the advent of the Concorde."

He also completed his postgraduate studies at INSEAD in Fontainbleau with the aid of a French government scholarship in 1982.

Chan elaborates on the cultural differences. "In the Singapore system, everything is geared towards pragmatism. The French, on the other hand, teach from first principles and students are asked to work from the abstract to the practical. Education is also very broad-based. Engineering students are required to study Philosophy and French Literature. Oral examinations take up 60 percent of the grades. The basis for this is that if an engineer cannot explain things to his technician or client, then he is not a good engineer."

Chan also has two illustrious siblings. His sister, Prof Chan Heng Chee, is currently Singapore's Ambassador to the USA. She was in the pioneering batch of Political Science students in the University of Singapore and created history by obtaining a First Class Honours in 1964. She was the founding Director of the Institute of Policy Studies, the founding Executive Director of the Singapore International Foundation and Director of the Institute of Southeast Asian Studies. His brother, Heng Wing, has served as Ambassador to Thailand and is currently Consul-General in Shanghai.

Heng Loon has a distinguished record of public service. He was Airport Manager with the Department of Civil Aviation (1980–1984) and was with the Singapore Administrative Service (1984–2002). His other positions included being MINDEF Director of Manpower, Principal Private Secretary to the then Senior Minister. He also served as Permanent Secretary in the Ministry of Communications (now known as the Ministry of Transport).

He made a successful career switch from public to private sector when he became the Deputy President and CEO of Singapore Press Holdings in 2002. "The public sector has a very structured decision-making system whereas in the private sector, things are more fluid. The emphasis on profitability is very important in the private sector, something not often discussed in the public sector."

Alan Chan Heng Loon is a Rafflesian who has crossed many boundaries, from the anglophone to the francophone worlds, from civil aviation to the administrative service and from the public to the private sectors.

A Star is Born

Kit Chan

Kit Chan's full name is Chan Kit Ee. As a schoolgirl, she loved to sing and act. She has often been credited to be the first Singaporean pop singer to break into the regional Chinese pop scene. A phenomenal recording star, she has been extensively featured in television and stage musicals. She has also published a book of poetry, and co-wrote a novel with her best friend from RGS. Besides her achievements in the field of entertainment, Kit Chan is also recognised as a trailblazer in humanitarian and youth work, becoming Youth Ambassador for the National Youth Council from 1998–2000, and then going on to win the Singapore Youth Award for Arts and Culture in 2001, and the Commonwealth Youth Programme Asia Award for Excellence in Youth Work in 2002. She served in the committee for NYC from 2001–2004, and currently serves as a board member on the National Heritage Board, as well as contributes to the Resource Panel for the MICA Government Parliamentary Committee.

She studied in Raffles Girls' School from 1985 to 1988. "I love singing. When I was in RGS, I practised singing daily with my friends." She took the unconventional path when she enrolled as a student at the LaSalle School of Drama. She caught the attention of a local record company when she sang advertising jingles while still pursuing her studies.

When she was twenty-two, Kit Chan took the bold decision to leave for Taiwan. "I'm not afraid of competition. If you want to create an impact on the international music scene, you have to go out of Singapore. If a singer makes it overseas, she will also succeed in her own country." Soon, her face was on the covers of Taiwanese entertainment magazines. They described her as a young talent with such a soulful voice that she seemed to be breathing life into each of her songs. In 1994, she hit the big time with her album *Heartache*. In the same year, she won the local 'Media Recommendation for Best New Artiste Award', which would be followed by many other awards and accolades, musical or otherwise.

Not content with just being a mega pop star, Kit Chan turned her attention to the stage. In 1997, she was cast alongside Asian megastars in the Cantonese musical *Snow.Wolf.Lake*. She won the crowd over, despite being a virtual unknown in Hong Kong. "I spent ten years in a pop career and I was tired of it. Musicals were what first attracted me to the stage. And I'm glad that I've had the chance to realise my dreams. *Snow.Wolf.Lake* will always have a special place in my heart." Kit was thus quoted in the later part of her performance career, as she veered towards more musicals.

What draws Kit Chan to musicals is the live element and camaradarie with fellow actors. "As a pop singer, you don't perform live often, apart from gigs and concerts. But in a musical, you're always having fun as a group, even if rehearsals are a drudgery." She went on to wow audiences in China with her solid vocals in the 2004 Mandarin version of *Snow.Wolf.Lake*. She opened the Esplanade in 2002, playing the formidable Empress Cixi in the English musical, *The Forbidden City: Portrait of an Empress*, which was commissioned by the Esplanade and staged by the Singapore Repertory Theatre. She also starred in the Taiwanese musical *What's Love About* in 2002 and 2003.

How does she see herself as an actress? In RGS, she played the Princess in *Aladdin and the Wonderful Lamp*, and Maria in *The Sound of Music*. "I have often wondered why I was chosen to play the Princess. I always wanted to play something more radical. I realised later that it was because I have a leading lady's voice. My voice is clear and somewhat sweet."

In 2004, Kit Chan publicly announced that she would be taking an indefinite break from the Chinese recording pop scene. Since then, she has been living the quieter lifestyle she craved, out of the public limelight. Other than a couple of choice projects a year (including the 2007 National Day theme song, *There's No Place I'd Rather Be*), she has taken the time to go back to school to earn a BA (Hons) in Popular Music, picked up French, and is currently planning a second career in a different field.

Still, the performance bug which she caught in RGS all those years ago is not about to leave Kit anytime soon. "I don't think I will ever stop singing. It is like asking me not to eat or breathe. I just don't think I will ever do it the way I did in my 20s and through to my early 30s. It won't be so demanding and driving. I will always love it, but I can't let it run my life. Life is short, and God knows I've given enough of it to being a professional performer and working to the point of not really having a life. I want to experience something else. I need to be challenged all over again!"

We hope she will continue to inspire and enchant us for many years to come.

Like Mother Like Daughter

Betty Chen

The name Betty Chen is synonymous with the Chinese Women's Association, which runs the Henderson Senior Citizens' Home, a sheltered home for the elderly, a torch which she has been carrying for her mother, May Wong, who was the Association's President for life.

Betty Chen was born in China and came to live in Singapore when her father became the Manager of the Bank of East Asia. She studied at Raffles Girls' School from 1933 to 1941. "I may never have been an old RGS girl, except for the persistence of my mother who was a very determined lady. After all, RGS was the best girls' school at that time and still is. The Principal told her that I was late for entering school and that there was no room for me. Undeterred, my mother walked to the classes and spotted an empty desk in one of the classrooms. She persuaded the teacher to put me there. So, I finally did end up being a RGS girl." Chen was also one of the first girls to study Science at Raffles Institution.

Three days before the fall of Singapore, her family boarded a ship bound for Australia. In the Java Sea, out of 24 ships that were bombed by Japanese planes, only three were not sunk. The ship they were on, the *Gorgon*, thankfully escaped. After a perilous journey, they finally reached Perth and safety. She graduated in Commerce from the University of Melbourne, where she met her architect husband. After the War, the couple settled in Singapore, then transferred to Kuala Lumpur in 1957 for 13 years before coming back to Singapore in 1969.

She was strongly influenced by her parents. Her mother, May Wong, was a native of Sacramento, California and was the only Chinese girl in her home town who went to school and college. She drove a car when she was only fourteen and when she came to Singapore, she became one of the first Chinese women to hold that distinction. She was a famous volunteer in community service for 50 years and a pioneer of women's emancipation. Her involvement in social work began in 1933, when she would go to the docks and rescue young girls who were brought from China and sold as cheap labour. As President of the Chinese Women's Association, she was in charge of the Henderson Senior Citizens' Home for the Elderly from 1978.

"I practically grew up with the CWA. When my mother died in 1989, I had to think very hard about her legacy. I thought that it was only right for me to continue her work. I felt that it was something she would have liked me to do. Now, I enjoy doing it because the old people are so appreciative and it means so much to them to have a safe home and be looked after."

Despite growing up with a silver spoon in her mouth, Chen points out that she had been exposed to the less privileged since she was young, learning from her parents. "I used to visit my old *amah* in Pagoda Street. I had also visited the old one-room HDB flats with their dark corridors. At the Henderson Home, we have changed the concept of homes for the elderly. The Home is clean, bright and cheerful." The Home, which accommodates 30 residents and has facilities for a social and a Lifestyle Centre, is solely funded by the CWA, which was the first Women's Voluntary Welfare Organisation to establish such a Home.

The CWA was founded in 1915, when women did not have much education. It encouraged women to acquire skills in cooking, sewing and music. Its members have included some of the most illustrious women in Singapore.

When her mother was the President, Betty Chen was content to play second fiddle. Now under her leadership, the CWA has expanded its services to cater to the needs of the elderly. She plays the lead role in fund-raising and overseeing the Henderson Home, and editing the CWA Journal. A tireless and ageless activist, she has survived breast cancer and has a zest for life. For a woman like Betty Chen, age does not come into the picture — only achievements, events and acts of charity.

Mr POSB

Bertie Cheng

Bertie Cheng Shao Shiong nearly became a teacher and a policeman. Instead, he devoted his whole working life to the postal service and became the Chief Executive Officer of the Post Office Savings Bank. Under his leadership, the POSB became the first local bank to computerise and introduce the ATM.

He was educated at Rangoon Road Primary and Raffles Institution. He is an Economics graduate of the then University of Malaya in Singapore. He was recruited into the Postal Services Department as the Assistant Comptroller of Posts.

Cheng had gone to the university on a teaching bursary. He was all set to become a teacher when he received a letter informing him of his appointment as an Assistant Superintendent of Police. "I knew myself and decided that I was not cut out to be a policeman." So he wrote back requesting an alternative. That was how he started his career with the postal services.

It was only in 1966 that he became involved with the POSB. He was picked to lead a 30-member team to the joint POSB Headquarters in Petaling Jaya, to bring back the ledger accounts of the Singapore POSB. The 250,000 ledger cards were transported back in three lorries. Cheng was with the POSB until his retirement in 1997, rising to General Manager and CEO. He remembers his tiny office in Middle Road, which was situated next to a bus stop. There was no air-conditioning and he had to work amidst all the noise and fumes.

The POSB originated with the idea of promoting the saving habit among school children who were encouraged to buy postage stamps and paste them on cards. In 1966, the bank had 250,000 depositors, rising to one million depositors by 1976. "It's a nice feeling to know that you have grown with the organisation."

Cheng is modest about his achievements and as he had always kept a low profile, there is hardly any mention of him in the media. "It has been a very interesting career. POSB is a very different kind of financial institution." Under his dynamic leadership, POSB was the first local bank to computerise, going online in 1974 and introducing ATMs in 1976. His greatest satisfaction was in the bank's ability to persuade more people to save and to witness its phenomenal growth. He pushed for the many innovations which made POSB the pacesetter in the industry. But, he never claimed any credit for them. "I always walked a few steps behind the Chairman."

He always stressed to his staff that they should be people-oriented. He motivated them, without wielding the big stick. The only thing which could upset him was if customer service was not met. He kept his meetings light-hearted, which made for a happy atmosphere.

Bertie Cheng's friends know him as a good storyteller, with a keen sense of humour. "I like to crack jokes, but I'm not a joker. I'm a mad man. M. A. D. stands for 'Make A Difference'. I try to make a difference. So I'm mad." His philosophy in life can be summed up by one of his favourite aphorisms. "Quitters don't win and winners don't quit."

Twinkletoes

Chia Boon Leong

Chia Boon Leong was born on New Year's Day in 1925. Only 5 foot 3 inches tall, this 80-year-old maestro is a legend in Singapore's football. He holds the double distinction of representing China in the 1948 Olympic Games in London and being a member of the victorious Singapore team which won the Malaya Cup 1950–1952.

As a boy, Chia learned to play football with the other *kampong* boys in Pasir Panjang, by kicking a tennis ball. In Raffles Institution, he was an outstanding athlete. Chia won fame with his dazzling skills and artistry with the ball. He was the scourge of the opposing teams' defence, mesmerising and waltzing round them with effortless ease. He was indeed the little magician with the deadly strike. The coach of the visiting Swedish team saw him in action and was very impressed by "that little fellow with the twinkling feet." From then on, the nickname of 'Twinkletoes' stuck.

Chia first represented Singapore at the age of 17, when the Japanese authorities organised 'goodwill' missions to Malaya. At twenty-two, he became the youngest member of the Malayan Chinese team which toured Southeast Asia and Shanghai.

He is the only Singaporean footballer to play in the Olympic Games — albeit for China. The 1950s were the golden years of Singapore football and the awesome trio of Chia Boon Leong, Awang Bakar and Aw Boon Seong spearheaded the Colony into the Malaya Cup Finals five times. Singapore was champion for three consecutive years from 1950–1952. Chia was voted Malaya's most popular Footballer in 1954 and was awarded a training course in Physical Education and with Arsenal.

His decision to hang up his boots at the age of 30 surprised and disappointed his many fans. "I could have played for a few years more. But I felt that it was time to make a graceful exit. The fans were very passionate in their support. They could either cheer you or boo you. So, I did not want to suffer the ignominy of being booed." It was time that he concentrated on his profession as a Senior Financial Executive at Rediffusion. For nine scintillating years, Chia Boon Leong had thrilled and enthralled thousands and had propelled Singapore football into a regional power.

Chia is modest about his achievements. "When I started, many people told me that I would never make it. This only made me more determined to succeed. Because of my small size, I had to strengthen my instinct for survival. I learned how to be trickier, fitter and faster to outwit my bigger opponents. Playing at inside-left, I was closely marked. I was also harassed, bullied and received many hard knocks. His modesty prevents him from making comparisons with present day standards of Singapore football. "Times have changed and soccer has also changed. Nowadays, the players are fitter and faster. The techniques have become more sophisticated. Modern training facilities are also readily available. Then, football enjoyed only amateur status. We were not remunerated and we played for the love of the game. We were proud to play for our club and for Singapore. Nevertheless, I am grateful to football and to my fans. Without them, I would not have been able to travel to so many places like Shanghai or London."

Chia was already a megastar in the 1950s even when there was no television. His stage was the Jalan Besar Stadium, which could only hold 20,000 of his adoring fans. For those of my generation, the nickname 'Twinkletoes' will always be etched in our memory. After all, Chia Boon Leong has been described as "the answer to the scientist's definition of perpetual motion."

A Woman of Many Parts

Claire Chiang

Claire Chiang See Ngoh is a woman of many parts. She has led an interesting life as a mother of three children, an entrepreneur, academic, author, champion of women's rights and family values, and a Nominated Member of Parliament. She attended Nan Hua Primary School and Raffles Girls' Primary School, followed by Raffles Girls' Secondary School before proceeding to the National Junior College and the University of Singapore, where she graduated with Honours in Sociology. She pursued her academic interest after marriage and achieved a Masters of Philosophy Degree in Sociology from Hong Kong University. She is multilingual, speaking easily in English, Mandarin and French, and numerous Chinese dialects.

With her dynamic personality, she is invariably the centre of attraction. She represents the Ideal Woman, with her eloquence, beauty and intellect. While these qualities have endeared her to many, others have found her presence intimidating. So does she see herself as a *femme fatale*? "Not at all. People often see us bigger than life. I see myself as someone ordinary, with a vision and dreams. I like people to remember me by my passion for the causes I am committed to. I have been very fortunate in the people I meet and in the opportunities which have been given to me."

Claire recalls her early childhood. "There were ten of us, in a two-room flat at Race Course Road. I made do with a monthly allowance of $25 during my university years. I worked during my vacations to get supplementary pocket money to buy more books and clothes. I gave tuition and, on one occasion, sold my hair for $25. Since then, my long hair has been my signature."

After graduating from university, she sojourned to Paris to study French. On her return, part of her job functions included translating business excerpts in the *Nanyang Siang Pao* for the Commercial Division of the French Embassy. She revealed how her husband, Ho Kwon Ping, had courted her on his motorbike. "Our courtship was harder work as we were both working." Their common interests bore fruit with the founding of Banyan Tree Hotels and Resorts in 1994. Claire founded the retail arm of the resorts, Banyan Tree Gallery, which works closely with village cooperatives and not-for-profit marketing agents to produce local crafts in order to sustain gainful employment for artisans. Originating in Phuket in Thailand, the Banyan Tree group now includes 22 resorts and hotels, 58 spas, 70 galleries and two golf courses.

Claire is a Council member of the Chinese Chamber of Commerce and Industry. She is one of the first two women to achieve this distinction after 89 years. Did she have to force her way into this male dominated institution? "It was due to the enlightened leadership of President Kwek Leng Joo who opened the door to women. We cannot force it, we have to take the opportunity to want to make a difference. Men value our contribution and they want to learn. It's a start, but it's still slow."

Claire's achievements include a book that she co-authored: *Stepping Out — The Making of Chinese Entrepreneurs*. The 47 lives portrayed in the volume were based on four years of her research. "I was awakened to an old Singapore that I never knew. Therefore, I was grateful for the pioneering effort in nation building by these early entrepreneurs."

As the Nominated Member of Parliament from 1997 to 2001, she consistently focused on social services, women's access to employment and educational opportunities, family values and the disadvantaged. How does Claire Chiang see her parliamentary contribution as a woman? "We have paved the way for younger women to follow and not to be afraid of politics or see it only as a male terrain. The fact is, women do add value by offering another perspective to national debate. The question is no longer if women should be a part of decision making in policy fixing. The way forward is to promote a culture of opportunity by working at our differences and finding common ground on national issues, regardless of gender."

Her current efforts include championing Corporate Social Responsibility (CSR). In addition to chairing Banyan Tree's CSR division, Claire is also the President of the national society promoting CSR among organisations in Singapore, Singapore Compact for CSR which is also the country representative for the United Nations Global Compact. Her role is to encourage more companies to embrace the value proposition that businesses do well by doing good in the areas of corporate governance, environmental protection and community engagement. Claire is also the Chairperson of Employer Alliance, a network of corporations committed to create an enabling work environment to enhance work life integration for women and men.

Claire Chiang, voted 'Woman of the Year' in 1998, enjoys her privileged position in the community. Coming from a humble background herself, she is always mindful that there are people with special needs. In her own inimitable way, she tries her level best in executing whatever that was placed before her, by committing to action plans and achieving outcomes.

From *Charpoy* to the Bench

Choor Singh

Choor Singh came from humble beginnings. The son of a watchman, he began his working life as a solicitor's clerk and rose to the top of the Judiciary as a Supreme Court Judge. He was also an authority on Sikh history and religion.

Born in India in 1912, Choor Singh came to Singapore at the age of eight. He attended Pearl's Hill Primary School and Outram Road School and, each day, walked six miles to and from school. In his autobiography, he wrote that "At Outram, my father was a watchman at a godown in Havelock Road. The five-foot way was our home. We slept there in our *manja* or *charpoy*, did our cooking and everything else there. We bathed at the road side stand-pipe and washed our clothes there. There were public latrines in those days. I had no table or chair to do my homework. I did some reading under the street light. Even in 1927, when I was in Standard 7 in RI, we were living in the five-foot way in a godown in Read Street. After attending Pearl's Hill Primary School and then Outram Road School, I went to RI, the one and only government secondary school in those days. I was there from 1926 to 1929, the year I passed my Senior Cambridge Examinations at the age of 18. This is because I had started school at the age of eight. I was in the top class. The standard of football at RI was very high and some of the boys in our first team found a place in the Singapore team. I played cricket for the school team. I remember with affection, some of the masters who taught me."

Unemployed after leaving school because of the Great Depression (1930–1934), he earned a living giving private tuition. His life took an unexpected turn when he was employed as a clerk by a lawyer, because of their common interest in cricket. However, he received a monthly salary of only $20. So he joined the general clerical service of the Straits Settlements Government with a monthly salary of $60. As fate would have it, he was posted to the Official Assignee's Chambers. After passing the Intermediate Law Examinations of London University, he was appointed as a Coroner with the handsome monthly salary of $850 which also came with a driver and car.

Choor Singh persevered with his Law studies and passed the Final Examinations of Gray's Inn. However, he could not be called to the English Bar because he could not comply with the requirements of keeping Dining terms. In 1949, when he presided at a Magistrate's Court, he caused quite a stir. "It was quite a sensation to see a Sikh sitting as a Magistrate. In fact, I was the first Indian to do so. Before that, Sikhs in police uniforms were the only Sikhs seen in the Courts."

In 1953, he was granted leave to attend his Dinners, and it took him three days to reach England. After making four trips in two years, he was finally called to the English Bar in 1955.

His illustrious career took him all the way to the Supreme Court in 1963, where he gave a total of 105 judgements in all. His forte was Criminal Law. During his time, appeals from the Court of Criminal Appeal were heard by the Privy Council in England and his judgements were never overturned. Justice Choor Singh was highly respected as a 'No Nonsense' judge. He was quick to appreciate a sound argument but quicker to jettison a flawed proposition. Despite his stern and uncompromising exterior, he was meticulously fair and firm, with a deep sense of justice and of his responsibilities.

After 17 years as a Supreme Court Judge and a total of 47 years of distinguished public service, Choor Singh retired in 1980. He found time for community service and co-founded the Khalsa Association. He was also the Vice-Chairman of the National Kidney Foundation and a member of the Presidential Council for Minority Rights. He had kept himself busy researching and writing books on Sikh history and religion. His book *The Lives of the Sikh Gurus* is a textbook for Sikh students.

Choor Singh achieved high judicial office against overwhelming odds, through sheer hard work, determination and opportunity. He is an inspiring example of a self-made man, who started his career as a solicitor's clerk and became a Supreme Court Judge.

Mr Accountant-General

Chua Kim Yeow

Chua Kim Yeow was not born with a silver spoon in his mouth. Yet, with only nine years of schooling, he rose to the top of his profession. He was Singapore's Accountant-General. His successful career is inspiring, as he achieved it through self-study, sheer hard work and determination.

Chua was born in 1926. His father was a stevedore sub-contractor to the Singapore Harbour Board and the family lived in Chinatown. He entered Gan Eng Seng School in 1933 and became its top student when he won the Lim Boon Keng Gold Medal. This enabled him to enter Raffles Institution in 1940. However, his secondary education was abruptly terminated by the Japanese Occupation which lasted from 1942 to 1945.

The Japanese forces had landed in Malaya in December 1941 and were intensively bombing Singapore, which was the British military fortress in the Far East. He says, "They started on 7 December 1941. Every time they dropped the bombs, we were rudely awakened at night. In the last two weeks of January 1942, no lessons were conducted in RI. It was the very first time that we experienced air raids and we did not know what to expect. Every time the sirens sounded, we ran and sought shelter in the trenches in the school field which we had dug earlier. They were waist deep and we had to crouch in them to avoid being hit by any shrapnel."

In the first few days of the Japanese Occupation, Chua was hounded into a concentration camp in Chinatown. He was detained for three days and was released after interrogation. His Japanese captors obviously thought he was too young to be a subversive, as he was only 16 years old then. Others were not so lucky. Some had unwittingly boarded the lorries with the promise of work and they never returned.

When Chua was seventeen, his father died, and he tried all kinds of jobs to eke out a living. After the Occupation, he could not return to school as he had to support his widowed mother and two siblings. Although he found work in a Dutch trading firm, he could not afford to go to the university.

Through conscientious self-study, he passed the London Matriculation Examinations in 1947. In 1953, he passed the examinations of the Association of Certified Accountants after enrolling for a correspondence course with the UK School of Accountancy. This gave him the qualifications which enabled him to apply for executive jobs. He started work in the Income Tax Department, and in 1956, was transferred to the Accountant-General's Department, where he rose to become Singapore's Accountant-General in 1961.

Chua retired in 1981. He has been appointed to various executive positions in government-linked financial institutions, including the Development Bank of Singapore and the Post Office Savings Bank. Under his leadership from 1979 to 1986, DBS increased its assets from $3 billion to $14.6 billion, becoming the largest bank in Singapore. Similarly, POSB deposits grew from $9 billion to $18 billion during his term there from 1986 to 1993. He also left a network of more than 600 ATMs spread throughout Singapore.

Chua Kim Yeow is a shining example of a self-made man. He learned Accountancy through self-study at a time when only the sons of wealthy parents had the privilege of obtaining the professional qualification by going overseas to the United Kingdom or Australia.

Pioneering Industrialist

Lionel Cresson

Lionel Cresson was the first Chairman of the Board of Governors of the Singapore Polytechnic. He was a pioneering industrialist, inventor and entrepreneur. As President of the Rotary Club, he launched the Rotary Tuberculosis Clinic at the Tan Tock Seng Hospital. He also initiated the UMS Fund. He possesses a distinguished record of community service and was a founder member and President of the Singapore Manufacturers Association and the Federation of Employers. He was also a Municipal councillor and a member of the Public Service Commission.

Cresson was born in Singapore in 1900. He studied at Raffles Institution and later qualified as a chemical engineer and rubber technologist in London. Beginning his career as an assistant chemist with the Singapore Rubber Works Ltd, he ended up becoming its Managing Director. He founded Cressonite Industries Ltd, which are the pioneers and manufacturers of technical rubber products. Several patented uses and processes of natural rubber, including road-paving blocks, rubber surfacing materials for floors and walls, rubber panes and roofing were invented by him.

Cresson was a pioneer in technical education. When he was appointed the first Chairman of the Board of Governors of the Singapore Polytechnic from 1955 to 1959, he had an impressive string of credentials behind him. He oversaw the building of the polytechnic at Prince Edward Road and the implementation of its courses and laid the foundation for it to develop into a modern institution of technology. One of the first things he did when becoming its Chairman was to organise a mission to visit polytechnics in England and Western Europe. "We want to learn from the mistakes of others and try to avoid making them ourselves."

As the President of the Rotary Club, Cresson is credited with the establishment of the Rotary Tuberculosis Clinic at the Tan Tock Seng Hospital. Singapore was then just recovering from the ravages of the Japanese Occupation. The majority of Singaporeans suffered from malnutrition, poor health and living conditions. Tuberculosis was rampant in Singapore and Rotary took on the challenge to eradicate the disease as a community service. In 1946, the idea of establishing the first tuberculosis clinic was mooted. Being such an important health project, it received government backing. The club was offered a site on the premises of Tan Tock Seng Hospital. The government also promised to match the club's fund-raising efforts, dollar for dollar. It took Lionel Cresson two years to complete the project and to raise $250,000, with the government adding another $250,000. It was known as the Rotary TB Clinic, which to this day is still in operation. It is now known as the Rotary Clinic as the word 'TB' has been dropped since the disease has been eradicated in Singapore. Thus Lionel Cresson's heroic pioneering role is forever enshrined in the clinic's existence. He also championed the cause of university education. Under his inspiring leadership, the Rotary Club organised a 'Movie Ball' and raised $17,500, which was donated to the university.

In the context of colonial Singapore, Lionel Cresson's many achievements were nothing short of genius. He was an intrepid inventor and a pioneer in manufacturing, in an entrepôt economy. A true Rafflesian, he used his wealth and influence to benefit the community, especially in the areas of public works, health and education. A philanthropist, he was the benefactor of many worthy causes, such as the Malaya Fund.

Of Trade and Diplomacy

Ridzwan bin Haji Dzafir

As an Ambassador-at-Large, Ridzwan bin Haji Dzafir belongs to the select company of only three Ambassadors in Singapore to be honoured with such a prestigious appointment. In his 46 years of distinguished public and community service, he has served as Deputy Secretary of the Ministry of Foreign Affairs, Director-General of the Trade Development Board and Non-Resident Ambassador to Argentina, Brazil, Chile and Panama. He is also a Pro-Chancellor of the NUS and a stalwart of the Malay community.

Ridzwan Dzafir was born in 1927 and grew up in the Kampong Glam area. He studied at the Kota Raja Malay School, Telok Kurau Primary and Raffles Institution. "I was one of the few Malay boys who succeeded to get into RI in 1940. My studies were interrupted by the Japanese Occupation. I helped out in my brother's restaurant and did work as an interpreter for a Japanese company, because I had studied in a Japanese school. I completed my Senior Cambridge in 1947 and I was the second boy in the school. I was given a scholarship to Raffles College. My friends and I were in our early twenties then. The War years had toughened us and we were mature students. Some of us became very political, inspired by the nationalist movements in Southeast Asia. It was a very interesting period. To supplement my studies, I also taught in the evenings."

Ridzwan graduated with a Bachelor of Arts from the then University of Malaya in Singapore in 1952. As he had to support his parents and siblings, he could not complete his Geography Honours year. His Civil Service career began in the Customs and Excise Department. "We spent some of the time catching smugglers." In 1961, he was promoted to a position in the Administrative Service. He was the Trade and Cultural Representative in Jakarta for two years and it was at the time when Indonesia began its Confrontasi with Malaysia. He was in the Malaysian Embassy when demonstrators ransacked it with cries of "Gantang Malaysia!"

When Singapore separated from Malaysia in 1965, he was posted to Kuala Lumpur to set up the Singapore Embassy. But soon he was shuttled back to Jakarta to set up the Singapore Embassy there. In 1968, he returned to the Trade Division and oversaw its transformation into the Trade Development Board. He became its Director-General, and for 16 years until his retirement in 1991, served in this position. He had learned to communicate with rubber and rice merchants in Hokkien and Teochew, and also developed the core of professional trade officers.

While he was in the Trade Development Board, Ridzwan was also Singapore's Non-Resident Ambassador to Argentina, Brazil, Chile and Panama from 1986 to 1997. He also served as the President of MUIS, the Malay religious council, and as the CEO of the Yayasan Mendaki. At the ripe old age of 78, he still leads a very active life carrying out his 16 official appointments, which include being the Pro-Chancellor of NUS and being in the Council of Presidential Advisers, and the Presidential Council for Minority Rights.

Ambassador-at-Large Ridzwan Dzafir provides an interesting insight into the role of diplomacy within ASEAN. He says, "Distinctly different cultures prevail in these countries. Colonial rule and communism have had a great impact on their respective systems and governance and the characteristics of the people. Different strategies have thus to be applied when engaging them in substantive discussions. The ASEAN family with a population of 500 million and rich in natural resources have the potential of becoming a powerful community in Asia. My involvement in ASEAN over many years has undoubtedly further enriched my diplomatic skills and have been an invaluable experience.

Ridzwan Dzafir is an inspiring example of a self-made man who has made a significant contribution to Singapore as well as internationally. Despite his humble background and the initial trauma of undergoing an English education, he became a top student at RI and in the university. He transformed the Trade Development Board from a mere trade division into an established national institution of commerce and industry. In the international diplomatic circuit, he is someone highly regarded for his modest and unassuming style of diplomacy.

Second Prime Minister

Goh Chok Tong

Goh Chok Tong is Singapore's second Prime Minister. He took over the helm of government at the age of 49. During his 14 years as Prime Minister, from 1990 to 2004, Singapore experienced many changes which were driven largely by external events. These included the ending of the Cold War, the primacy of American power, the Asian financial crisis and the imminent global competition posed by China and India. He became Senior Minister in 2004.

Goh was born in 1941. He was educated at Pasir Panjang Primary and received his secondary education at RI from 1955 to 1960. He was a good scholar and sportsman as well as a prefect, Scout troop leader, school swimming captain and the editor of *The Rafflesian.* As chairman of the Historical Society, he had his first classic encounter with Singapore's first Prime Minister, when he presided over a talk addressed by Mr Lee Kuan Yew.

Goh had a distinguished academic record and graduated with First Class Honours in Economics from the University of Singapore in 1964. He obtained his Masters in Development Economics from Williams College in 1967. In the one-hour interview with him at the Istana, Goh Chok Tong was very relaxed as we shared many pleasant memories of our friends and teachers in Raffles and the university. He poignantly recalled how he had lost his father when he was only 10 years old. "He told me to study hard and to take care of my mother and my younger siblings. I have always kept my promise to him. His death spurred me to undertake my responsibilities in earnest. Some of my classmates are now my friends for life. My most inspiring teacher was Mr Philip Liau. He nurtured my love for Literature with his artistic sketches of Shakespearean characters on the blackboard. He also recommended that I should be the Head Prefect to the Principal. But the Head Prefect was elected, for the first time, by the whole school and I lost to my closest friend."

In the university, he qualified for Triple Honours to read English, Geography and Economics. His life would have taken a different course, if he had not read Economics. Singapore would have been the poorer also. He joined the Administrative Service in 1964 and served in the Economic Planning Unit. In 1969, he joined Neptune Orient Lines as its Planning and Projects Manager, rising to become the Managing Director (1973–1977).

Goh Chok Tong was elected as the Member of Parliament for the Marine Parade Constituency in 1976. His entry into politics was initiated by the Finance Minister, the late Mr Hon Sui Sen, who explained that the PAP leadership was undergoing a process of self renewal and that they were grooming bright young men to replace the 'old guards'. "Hitherto, I had no real interest in direct Party politics, although I had followed local current events closely. I agreed to stand for election, for two reasons. Firstly, a sense of obligation. I went to the university through a bursary. So I had to give something back. Secondly, I had thought that the PAP had enough capable people to be ministers. I then realised that since they had asked me, they must be short of people. I never had any inkling that I would end up as the Prime Minister. The only possibility I had thought of was that I would end up as the Finance Minister." He held various ministerial posts, including those in Trade and Industry, Health and Defence (1979–1991). He was also appointed First Deputy Prime Minister in 1985.

At the age of 49 when he succeeded Lee Kuan Yew, Goh Chok Tong became Singapore's second Prime Minister on 28 November 1990. He frankly admits that he had to give the exalted position very serious thought and had finally accepted it with some apprehension. Mr Lee had posed the question to him and a few others who were in the running for the premiership, as to what would happen to Singapore after his departure. "He was concerned about Singapore's stability and continuity, particularly from the point of view of foreign investors.

I never thought of assuming the post of Prime Minister. I was asked to do the job by my colleagues and they assured me of their support and their confidence in me. So in my own mind, I told myself that if I could keep Singapore going, after Lee Kuan Yew, I would have done my part for Singapore. Serving Singapore is the greatest honour of my life. Also, I never think of my legacy. If you keep thinking of your legacy, your colleagues will say this chap is only looking after his own interests." At Cabinet meetings, he always strove to build consensus.

He is characteristically modest, almost self-effacing, when reminded of his many achievements. He created the Government Parliamentary Committees (GPCs), Town Councils and Community Development Councils. He also initiated schemes, such as the upgrading of HDB flats, Edusave, Medisave, CPF top-ups and the Asset Enhancement Scheme. He reinforced Singapore's status within ASEAN and internationally. He initiated Free Trade Agreements, enabling Singapore to link up with major world economies.

Citing his own example, he has this inspiring message for Singaporeans. "You can be whatever you aspire to be. The opportunities are there. The door is open. There are no hurdles in front of you."

Goh Chok Tong has no immediate plans to write his memoirs to perpetuate his name in history. "I'm just doing my part for the country. I want to ensure that people coming after me can keep this place going. I have a happy and balanced life. Well, that's good enough for me."

Goh Chok Tong relinquished his post as Prime Minister of Singapore on 12 August 2004 after 14 years. He was then appointed Senior Minister and also became the Chairman of the Monetary Authority of Singapore.

World Famous Dancer and Choreographer

Goh Choo San

Goh Choo San achieved international fame as the resident choreographer of the famous Washington Ballet. When he died of viral colitis at the relatively young age of 39, he bequeathed a legacy of US$500,000 for the development of young dancers and choreographers.

He was born in 1948, and while studying at Raffles Institution, already showed his talent for dance. He received his earliest dance training from his older brother and sister who had studied ballet in London. After graduating in Biochemistry from the University of Singapore in 1970, he left for Europe to further his ballet career, starting out as a dancer with the Dutch Ballet where he began choreographing in earnest.

According to his friends, Goh was a highly-strung youth, who came to life only when he was dancing or choreographing. He looked the very image of the leading, lethargic, languid loner who liked to spend his time at home, listening to Stravinsky, Debussy and Rabael. He had an artistic eye for fashion, an invaluable asset when it came to costuming dancers. And he was a collector of objects of art and especially fond of Chinese embroidery and painting.

Although he had no musical training, he was one of the most musical of his profession. His works were characterised by the tasteful blending of his Asian roots with Western technique. In 1976, he became the resident choreographer of the Washington Ballet. He was prolific, creating five works yearly and in the next eight years, he added

37 ballets to his name, which brought him international recognition. Ironically, he was not acknowledged at home until 1987, when he was awarded the Cultural Medallion. He lamented how he had to seek his fame and fortune elsewhere. "I hated Singapore. It was so stifling artistically. There's no time for the artist, no subsidies. Nothing but work and business. There's little respect for the dancer."

His work received rave reviews and his rise was meteoric. Within a decade, he soared to celebrity status on the wings of his creations. His ballets were marked by a first rate command of structure and fluency, concentrating on speed, intricacies of movement, difficult toework and streamline partnering. His famous works included *Configurations, In the Glow of the Night* and *Romeo and Juliet.* He also played a role in the formation of the Singapore Dance Theatre and the Singapore Ballet Academy.

A genius in his profession, he was a perfectionist and a hard taskmaster. But he also had humility and humanity. "I have no pipe dreams. I don't believe life is fair. I let it dictate wherever I go. I don't think about tomorrow. It is the moment which matters most. I get pleasure from my work, not because it's mine, but because it's exciting, because it's good and because it moves me."

When Goh Choo San died in 1987 at thirty-nine, he was approaching the height of his fame. *The Washington Post* described his death as "a loss of incalculable magnitude." He had been philosophical about his illness. "The more at ease you are with yourself, the easier it is to face death."

On Top of the Banking World

Euleen Goh

Euleen Goh reached the pinnacle of her profession after some 21 years in banking. She is the second Singaporean woman to hold the top post of CEO of Standard Chartered Bank. In that, too, she was responsible for driving the Bank's corporate governance and strategic agenda in Singapore. She is also the Non-Executive Chairman of International Enterprise Singapore, an agency under the Ministry of Trade and Industry whose mission is to help Singapore-based companies grow and internationalise successfully.

Euleen Goh received her primary and secondary education at Singapore Chinese Girls' School. She was active in athletics and in the Girl Guides and was the captain of the school netball team. She then proceeded to Raffles Institution (1972–1973) where she captained the volleyball team. "The biggest impact RI had on me was my fellow students, not necessarily those who had material wealth, but those who were rich in their friendships with other students, in their academic accomplishments and in their association with the values of the school. My first months in a co-ed school were interesting in terms of having to learn to be much more circumspect with boys and how to engage with them. Today, looking back, I'm proud to be associated with a school that has nurtured so many leaders who have answered the call to serve the nation."

As a Science student, the young Euleen enjoyed the logic of Mathematics. As her ambition was to be a chartered accountant, she took the fastest route into the profession via a five-year study and work programme, which included a one-year stint at the Oxford Polytechnic. She is also grateful to her parents for developing her sense of independence as she had to leave for England at the age of 19. A chartered accountant, she also holds professional qualifications in banking and taxation.

"I worked in Stanchart for 21 years and climbed the career ladder progressively during that time. The first decade was important, particularly my experiences in overseas markets. I could draw on them when I assumed the leadership role in the bank. I was also posted to London and I was one of the few Singaporeans who were prepared to be posted overseas. As the bank's CEO, I was the community link to ensure that the bank and our staff played a value-added role for the community and the success of Singapore's economy. The long term future of our country is important to us and we should all play our part as corporate citizens."

Euleen Goh is modest about her achievements in the predominantly man's world of banking. "It is a key highlight to me that there were so many caring people who made a big difference in my career. Generally, Singapore men can still be very intimidated by powerful career women. Our social norms still expect the male to be the breadwinner. However, the world is far more open today. There are bankers who have the *wow* factor. They are the life and soul of the party. I was not one of them and I didn't think that I would be good at the party and cocktail circuit. Nevertheless, I adapted my skills and ended up enjoying it immensely because I had to deal with people."

Her expertise is very much in demand. Her list of community service includes MediaCorp, Financial Standards Committee and the Institute of Banking and Finance. Under her inspiring leadership, Stanchart has been the benefactor of the Singapore Association for the Blind, HIV Aids and other charities.

Unlike most CEOs, Euleen Goh does not stay in five-star resorts when she is on vacation. In keeping with her adventurous spirit, she mountain treks and hikes in the Himalayas and New Zealand. She also takes walks at the MacRitchie Reservoir and climbs Bukit Timah Hill. She is always mindful of the demands on young Singaporeans. "We are a fairly elitist society. You've got to have the right grades from young and must also be outstanding and have leadership qualities."

Euleen Goh, the trailblazer for women in the banking world has the last word. “I always tell people that I am an ordinary person. I enjoy my life. I managed to get into good schools. You can still do well in life from an ordinary background. If I can do it, so can you too.”

Newspaper Editor

Han Fook Kwang

Han Fook Kwang had his first taste of journalism, when he was a schoolboy. He loved reading and writing. Although he graduated in Mechanical Engineering, he did not practise Engineering. Instead, he served in the Administrative Service working on public policies. His first love was journalism and he yearned to make it his profession. Now, as the Editor of Singapore's largest selling daily newspaper, he has come full circle.

Han studied at Presbyterian Primary and RI (1966–1971). He was a Scout, school photographer and managing editor of *The Rafflesian Times*. It was the only student newspaper in Singapore, which was self-financing. "The biggest challenge was to get advertisements. We pounded the streets along Shenton Way and knocked on office doors. It also had to be good enough for students to buy. So it was a wonderful preparation for the real thing." He also recalls that he was fortunate to be staying near the Joo Chiat library. "I had my first library card at the age of seven. It was a fascinating experience to see so many books and to borrow them free of charge. I was able to read many examples of very good writing. When I was in pre-university, I became interested in philosophy and my favourite author was Bertrand Russell because he wrote so logically and lucidly."

He graduated in Mechanical Engineering from Leeds University in 1975 with the aid of a Colombo Plan Scholarship. "In the 1970s, Engineering was in vogue. Without the scholarship, I would not be able to proceed to university abroad." He also obtained his Masters in Public Administration from Harvard. He was bonded to the Civil Service from 1979–1987, where he served mainly in the Ministry of Communications, handling transport policies. He also had brief spells of work with Labour, the Economic and Development Board, and SGH. "I wasn't sure that I wanted to spend the rest of my life in the Civil Service. I was always keen on writing. So I decided to take the plunge into journalism and joined *The Straits Times* in 1989." Thus he began his new career as a senior leader and feature writer, after that as Political Editor and finally as Editor in 2002.

Han Fook Kwang co-authored with two other journalists the book *Lee Kuan Yew, The Man and His Ideas*. "We had 13 interviews, on Saturday afternoons, each lasting about 90 minutes. Minister Mentor is meticulous and very thorough. He also has a fantastic memory. We uncovered the fact that the first political speech Mr Lee made was on behalf of a Labour Party candidate at a British General election when he was an undergraduate at Cambridge."

Han has seen many changes in *The Straits Times*. "When I first joined, we were a black and white paper. We introduced colour in the early 1990s and have redesigned the paper a few times, including its masthead. These days the visual aspects — the colour, graphics and photographs — are very important. In the past, there wasn't so much competition for people's time. There was no television or Internet and not such a proliferation of newspapers. Now there are all these sources, all competing for the readers' attention. So, we need to offer more to readers than just telling them the news." He is confident that *The Straits Times* can stand up to most of the regional newspapers. "Our ambition is to be one of the top English language newspapers. We have an extensive network of correspondents covering Asia. We have received favourable comments for our reporting on Indonesia and Malaysia."

Han is aware that some of the world's newspapers are owned by powerful Press barons with vested interests, who could influence their editorial policies. "Some people say that *The Straits Times* is part of the government. However, SPH is a public-listed company and it is not government-owned. Editorial independence and credibility are very important assets of a newspaper. We sell about 390,000 copies of *The Straits Times* every day. Readers believe what they read in *The Straits*

Times, and we work very hard to maintain this so that we continue to be credible to our readers."

Han accepts the long hours in his office as part of his job. As Editor, he chairs three meetings daily to decide on the important line-ups. "We work to a deadline every day. We send the paper to bed at 1.30 am but the stories have to be done by midnight. A journalist's job is also unpredictable as you never know when a major news break will happen. When it does, you'll have to put everything else aside."

Han Fook Kwang, the consummate journalist, still speaks of his first love with pride and passion, after 18 years. "It's a wonderful human creation, the act of writing. It's one of the most creative human activities, and it's still magic to me."

Of Bricks and Mortar

Albert Hong Hin Kay

Albert Hong Hin Kay is a very successful architect as can be seen by his various projects, nationally and internationally. A self-made man, he is someone who donates his money generously to the arts and education, and is easily the biggest single benefactor of Raffles Institution. He was the first professional to win the 'Businessman of the Year Award'. He is quite comfortable with his dual role as a successful professional and a wealthy businessman.

He studied at Outram Primary School and Raffles Institution from 1950 to 1953 where he participated in many extra-curricular activities. From an early age, he learned to fend for himself. "Sometimes, I walked to school instead of travelling by bus, so that I could save ten cents to spend during recess. I think we played more than we studied. We also played truant so that we could see a show at the Capitol." The Japanese Occupation, during which time his family had to survive on tapioca and sweet potatoes, had a profound influence on him. It toughened him up for his studies in Architecture at Birmingham University. "My parents gave me a monthly allowance of £20. So I worked part-time in an ice cream factory and in Chinese restaurants. I sacrificed my holidays and managed to earn £400 annually, supporting myself through the five-year course and could even own a Ford car. My father taught me that hard work never killed anyone."

It was his stint with the Singapore Improvement Trust (SIT) which had convinced the 18-year-old Albert to become an architect. "When I was doing surveying work for the SIT, I saw six to seven people crammed into one room. I was determined to be an architect to improve those living conditions."

Hong returned to Singapore and began his career with an architectural practice. He was posted to Malacca for two years. The firm was renamed RSP Architects, Planners and Engineers Pte Ltd in 1992 when Hong became its Chairman and Managing Director. When he first joined the firm, there were only 14 employees. Today, the Group employs 600 people, of whom 500 are based in Singapore, making it the largest architectural practice in the Asia Pacific region. RSP adopts a multidisciplinary approach to business, offering clients a one-stop convenience, not only in design and planning, but also in civil, electrical, mechanical and structural engineering, as well as construction management and interior decoration.

Some of his overseas projects are tied up with government-linked companies, and local projects have included the MAS Centre.

In 1994, Hong was named 'Businessman of the Year', the first professional to win the award, which was given in recognition of his vision and outstanding ability in transforming his architectural practice into a leading regional corporation, and for his achievement as a professional turned businessman. Hong is quite comfortable with the apparent contradiction in terms. "You can't draw a fine line between the two. If you want to be a successful professional, you've got to think like a businessman." His formula for success is to have "the right people, the right team in the right place at the right time."

He may be seen as a hard-headed businessman. But he also has a big heart. His loyalty to his *alma mater* is exemplary in his donation of $2 million dollars to RI, and the school hall bears his name. He also donated $250,000 to the Tan Swan Beng Professorship at the Nanyang Technological University. Many artistic and educational institutions have also benefitted from his generosity. "I award scholarships to students with no strings attached. But I will expect them to give back to the community so that others can benefit." Hong has received several national awards for his contributions to public housing and to the construction industry.

Albert Hong Hin Kay has risen from humble beginnings to the pinnacle of his profession. He has successfully combined his professional ability with his business acumen, cemented by hard work and perseverance. He is an inspiring example of an entrepreneur with a social conscience.

Singapore's First President

Yusof Ishak

As a schoolboy, Yusof Ishak dreamt of becoming a soldier but this was overtaken by his love of journalism. He pioneered the founding of the *Utusan Melayu* and became a legend in the Malay community. His vision was a multiracial nation and this was realised when he became Singapore's First President in 1959.

He had three illustrious brothers. Abdul Aziz was a Head Prefect of Raffles Institution and became Malaya's first Minister for Agriculture. Rahim was the Minister of State for Foreign Affairs, and Mohammed was the Chairman of the Labour Party. But Ishak achieved the highest honour by being a Head of State.

Yusof Ishak was born on 12 August 1910 of Minangkabau descent in Padang Gajah, Perak, the eldest of nine children. His father, a civil servant, had been transferred to Singapore and was an Inspector of Fisheries. The family lived in the government quarters in MacNair Road.

He received his primary education at Telok Kurau School. In Raffles Institution, he was a brilliant all-rounder with that rare combination of brains and brawn. He was the classic example of the school's great tradition of scholastic and sporting excellence. He excelled in hockey, cricket, swimming, water polo and boxing. He was also Singapore's Light-Weightlifting Champion. Ishak was the first schoolboy to hold the rank of 2nd Lieutenant in the National Cadet Corps. In 1927, he passed his Cambridge School Certificate Examinations with distinction and was admitted into the Queen's Scholarship Class. He was also a prefect and co-editor of *The Rafflesian.*

After leaving school, he started *The Sportsman* and was the manager of *Warta Malaya*. In 1938, he established *Utusan Melayu*, the Malay language daily newspaper. It was owned, financed and staffed by Malays, and it was in the Arabic-Jawi script.

Yusof fervently argued the need for a truly Malay newspaper that would reflect the views, interests and aspirations of the Malays. Initially, 400 subscribers paid $2 per share. Strenuous efforts were made to raise the $10,000 needed. Ishak was its Chief Editor and Managing Director for 21 years. Under his inspiring leadership, the *Utusan* became the leading paper in Malaya. It was also a profitable concern. Ishak's dedication was legendary. During the Japanese bombings, he refused to leave his desk to ensure that the paper would be printed as scheduled. His editorial policy was Malay-Muslim oriented, but progressive, modernist and multiracial. He believed that education was the solution to the problems of the Malay community. Ishak became controversial for his commitment to multiracialism and racial equality. In 1950, the *Utusan* was put to the test during the Maria Hertogh riots. While presenting her case, it refrained from fanning the flames of hatred and emotion.

The progressively socialist slant of the *Utusan* had set it on a collision course with the United Malays National Organisation, whose members were buying up shares of the *Utusan* and attempting to bring it under their control. Ishak resisted but to no avail. In 1959, he left *Utusan*, his brainchild and life's work for 21 years. He had made great sacrifices and it was a sad end, but greater glory and responsibility was waiting for him.

The PAP won the General Election and formed the government. Ishak was soon appointed the Chairman of the Public Service Commission. On 3 December 1959, he became the Yang di-Pertuan Negara, Singapore's first Head of State. He was a very popular choice, because of his nationalist record and impeccable credentials. He realised that he was in the best position to encourage the Malays to find their rightful place together with the Chinese and Indians in Singapore. His first task was to create the office and image of the Head of State. He moved away from pomp and pageantry and presented himself as a humble, modest man, proud of his Malay roots, dedicated to the ideal of multiracialism. Together with his wife, Puan Noor Aishah, they formed a gracious couple, much respected and loved by the people.

On 9 August 1965, following the separation of Singapore from Malaysia, Yusof Ishak was installed as the First President of the Republic of Singapore. He played a crucial role in healing the wounds of separation and racial acrimony, particularly in 1969, when there were racial riots in Malaysia.

Despite the heavy demands of his office, Ishak had time for two hobbies — photography and orchids. One orchid hybrid, *Dendrobium Noor Aishah,* is named after his wife.

Yusof Ishak died on 23 November 1970. During his one decade of inspiring leadership, Singapore gained Independence. He was a nationalist, who honoured multiracialism as his creed. His death was deeply mourned by the whole nation. He was buried in the State Cemetery in Kranji.

Yusof Ishak has earned for himself a special place in the hearts and minds of Singaporeans, who will always remember him as a great and dedicated President. To Rafflesians, he will always be the inspiring example and embodiment of the school motto *'Auspicium Melioris Aevi'.*

Judicious Deputy Prime Minister

S. Jayakumar

Shanmugam Jayakumar became the Deputy Prime Minister, after 24 years in politics. As a schoolboy and an undergraduate, he had already shown that he had leadership qualities. This was useful preparation for his political career to come.

He studied at Rangoon Road Primary School, and Raffles Institution from 1953 to 1958 where he excelled in drama and inter-school debates. He acted in Shakespearean and other plays. He pays tribute to Mr Philip Liau, who was the driving force behind *The Raffles Players*. "The memories are not so much the play itself, but the organisation which went behind it. We had a lot of fun getting the props, selling tickets and printing programmes."

Jayakumar's decision to study Law was based on whether he should become a professional or whether he would find a job as an employee. In 1959, he was admitted to the Law Faculty of the University of Malaya (then in Singapore) and developed an interest in Constitutional and International Law. That was why he pursued an academic career rather than practise as a lawyer. He was the editor of the *Malayan Undergrad* and Chairman of the Students Council. "At that time, the Council was working closely with the Nantah students, in initiating the possible formation of a National Union of Students. Naturally, when you are a student councillor, you would tend to have an over-inflated sense of the importance of current issues. It was a good balance for my studies."

After his graduation, he joined the staff of the Law Faculty and pursued his postgraduate studies at Yale Law School where he obtained his Masters. He became Dean of the Law Faculty from 1971 to 1974. He was then appointed as Singapore's Permanent Representative to the United Nations. "I had thought that I would resume my academic career, when I returned to Singapore. It was then that I was approached to go into politics. It was not an easy decision and I discussed it with my wife and close friends."

Jayakumar was elected on a People's Action Party ticket as the Member of Parliament for the Bedok constituency in 1980. It later became a GRC (Group Representation Constituency). "It was put to me that the PAP was looking for a new team and that I was among the top in the list of names. If I declined then, they would have to go down the list. And if everybody said 'no', what will happen? And I will regret it." He gives an interesting insight into the life of an MP. "You have to deal with a cross-section of society. You have to give enough time to listen to problems. The key is really for them to know that you are paying attention to what they are saying. You have to be accessible, more so these days with the advent of the e-mail."

Jayakumar was Minister for Home Affairs and also for Law in 1988. During his term of office, he took tough actions to deal with illegal gambling, drug addiction and national security. "In any portfolio dealing with law and order, it means that you have to tackle some nasty situations. I received nasty letters. But that goes with the job. You cannot be affected by that."

Jayakumar was appointed the Foreign Minister in 1994. "It was originally set by the founding fathers. It is not something which is suddenly created. They had to set the key ingredients of how Singapore presents itself to the outside world. My role is to help evolve this policy. But because the world and the region kept changing, our foreign policy is never static. What is always constant is the advancement of Singapore's interests. Therefore the job of a Foreign Minister is to ensure that Singapore's interests are protected and advanced *vis-a-vis* the external environment, especially in the light of geo-political realities." He was appointed as Deputy Prime Minister in 2004. While still retaining the Law Minister's portfolio, he looks after Singapore's homeland security which cuts across several Ministries.

Jayakumar comes across as someone who is acutely conscious of the responsibility of high office. He is thorough, articulate and judicious.

Jayakumar has had a very distinguished career as a law professor and as a government minister. He admits that he had no burning ambition to be a politician. Nevertheless, like a true Rafflesian, he had heeded the call to render public service. Just as he took to the stage when he was a schoolboy, he has played a very prominent role on Singapore's political stage.

Shanmugam Jayakumar has the last word. "A school and its teachers play an important role in shaping one's approach to life. So looking back on my years in Raffles, they did have a major influence in my life."

The Architect in Nation Building

Hijjas Kasturi

Hijjas Kasturi is an internationally renowned architect. Some people say that the award-winning architect is an idealist while others say he is a visionary and a controversial thinker. It is an undeniable fact that through his buildings and patronage, Hijjas Kasturi has contributed significantly towards shaping a Malaysian identity and building a new nation. A philanthropist and a firm believer in education, he founded his own residency programme to support young architects, artists and writers.

Born in 1936, Hijjas describes himself as a *kampong* boy. Moving from Malay to Japanese schools during the Japanese Occupation, his schooling had a chequered start. He was the only student from Tanjong Rhu Primary to gain admission to RI. He soon displayed his prodigious talent in art when he was the artist for his class magazine. In 1955, he completed his Senior Cambridge Examinations. He frankly admits that he owes his success in his adult life to his *alma mater*.

"Raffles taught me character. The RI pursuit for scholastic excellence was ingrained in me, along with the competitive drive to be the best. It remains pivotal in my work practice today. Education is about building a future. It should nurture curious minds, instil a sense of purpose and personal drive, and celebrate achievements. Somehow, I could never quite fit the mould. For some reason, I wanted to do something that wasn't the norm. That has always been my hallmark, I suppose. My successful admission to RI was the turning point in my life," Hijjas reminisces nostalgically.

While at Raffles, he supported his schooling by working at night as a reporter for the *Melayu Raya*, which was later banned by the British authorities. His lessons at RI were juxtaposed with those learned at the newspaper. He soon realised that life was hard and he was also acutely aware of the politics and nationalism of the times. The independent struggles in Indochina, Indonesia and Malaya inspired him at a crucial impressionable age. The combination of the two shaped his mature intellect and sense of self, and have found echoes in the designs of his buildings.

It was in RI that Hijjas decided to become an architect and took his first decisive step to realise his ambition. He worked as a draughtsman with the Singapore Improvement Trust, gaining useful experience by studying the building plans. He seized his golden opportunity when he applied for a Colombo Plan Scholarship. It was the chance of a lifetime which completely changed the course of his life. He made strenuous preparations, borrowing books from libraries and appeared at the interview, confidently armed with his models and drawings. The panel was very impressed and decided that he was the best candidate and Hijjas was awarded the scholarship to study Architecture and Town Planning at the University of Adelaide. On returning to Singapore in 1966, he worked with the Housing and Development Board.

Hijjas, the bright young man, soon sought his fame and fortune in Malaysia. In 1967, he became the founding Head of the School of Art and Architecture at the MARA Institute of Technology. This continues to be one of his passions today — that of fusing art and architecture. He founded the Hijjas Kasturi Associates in 1972. The early projects of the 70s were mainly educational. In 1979, he won the competition sponsored by Malayan Banking, which was a significant point in his career.

Over the past 28 years, Hijjas Kasturi's vision of a Malaysian identity has become a reality in the buildings which bear his trademark, including Tabung Haji in 1986, Securities Commission Headquarters in 1999, and Menara Telekom in 2002. Commissioned to re-plan Singapore's Kampong Glam, Hijjas has now come full circle. It is with a sense of *déjà vu* he is revisiting the area from which he once cycled to school at RI. He continues to expand his vision in Malaysia, in the region, and in Saudi Arabia, Dubai and Mecca. "As architects, we have the tools to shape our cities with a sense of place and character." For his remarkable contributions to the architecture of Malaysia and to nation building, he was awarded the Gold Medal by the Malaysian Architecture Professional Institute. He has also received several international awards, as well as an honorary doctorate from the University of Malaya in 2005.

Hijjas Kasturi is modest about his outstanding achievements. Always conscious of his own humble beginnings, he is a philanthropist of the arts and education. He established, with his wife, Angela, his residency programme for young talents in the grounds of Rimbun Dahan, his home.

The Student's Principal

Khoo Kay Chai

Khoo Kay Chai has the distinction of being the first Singaporean Principal of the Singapore Polytechnic. For 30 years, he was the driving force and chief engineer of its growth and development. Under his capable and dynamic leadership, the Singapore Polytechnic was transformed from a mere technical institute into a modern institute of technology. When he retired in 1995, it had a staff of 1,500 and a student population of 15,000. Of the five polytechnics in existence today, Singapore Polytechnic remains the top choice of students.

Born in 1935, Khoo comes from a banking family and his grandfather was the first General Manager of the Overseas Chinese Banking Corporation and the first Managing Director of United Chinese Bank (now UOB). But Khoo was only interested in Engineering. He was enrolled at Gan Eng Seng Primary School but the Japanese Occupation from 1942 to 1945 prevented him from commencing his studies. He subsequently became the top boy of Gan Eng Seng School and had hoped to proceed to Raffles Institution, but this coincided with the GESS conversion into a secondary school. His Principal strongly urged him and his classmates not to leave the school. So Khoo had to wait another four years before he was admitted to the Post School Certificate class of Raffles Institution in 1955.

Khoo graduated in Engineering from the University of Malaya in 1961. The newly-established Engineering Faculty was based in Kuala Lumpur. He recalls exciting memories of boarding the Malayan Railway train to Kuala Lumpur, and returning to Singapore for the holidays. He started his career as an engineer with the Public Works Department.

Later, he decided to switch to Education and was appointed to the post of assistant lecturer with the Civil Engineering Department of the Singapore Polytechnic in 1965. When he took charge of the newly-opened Ayer Rajah campus with 2,000 students, he proved his administrative ability and was promoted to Principal in 1978. He was directly responsible for speeding up the production of technicians for Singapore's then fledgling industrialisation programme. He had the unenviable task of providing places for school-leavers in the 1980s when there were insufficient technical training institutes. "The experience of steering Singapore to rise to the needs of the nation was meaningful and enriching. We worked very closely with the multinational corporations and factories who needed our graduates very rapidly and in large numbers. They also filled vital posts in the HDB, Singapore Telecoms, PUB and SIA. Many of our graduates have also gone abroad and obtained degrees. The more adventurous have gone into business and become entrepreneurs employing university graduates."

Since its founding 50 years ago, Singapore Polytechnic has produced more than 100,000 graduates. "The polytechnic has to find a new role. In the past, it played a vital role in serving the needs of Singapore's industrialisation programme. Our manpower needs have changed. We are no longer in the phase of setting up factories for manufacturing. The country is looking for new ventures and new economic activities. Its basic role is to train our manpower skills. The more difficult part is for the polytechnic to assist in identifying these new activities."

As an educator, Khoo Kay Chai takes umbrage with those who label certain students as 'dropouts'. He believes that education should be broad-based so that every young person can be encouraged to develop his talents and skills to realise his full potential.

Very much the students' Principal, Khoo Kay Chai always held his students' welfare close to his heart. He initiated several schemes to generate an *esprit de corp* among the young men and women, and to create a unique Singapore Polytechnic identity. He set up the Continuing Education Department to look after the affairs of part-time students. He introduced the Advanced Diploma courses to cater for the polytechnic graduates who have aspirations beyond their polytechnic diploma. He also started the Personal Tutor Network to strengthen teacher-student rapport and launched the Graduates Guild House in the polytechnic grounds. The Career and Guidance Centre, the Entrepreneurs Club, and the Singapore Polytechnic anthem are among his legacy. He also encouraged the growth of student clubs and societies.

Khoo Kay Chai can look back with pride on his pioneering role in transforming the Singapore Polytechnic into the top-notch technological institution of our nation.

From Bukom to Lumut

Khoo Tee Chuan

As Khoo Tee Chuan studied British Empire history in his school lessons, he was held spellbound by the adventures of Sir Francis Drake and how the British navy defeated the Spanish Armada. But his love for the sea was not only confined to books. Living in Pulau Bukom, he was fascinated by the ships plying the Singapore harbour as he was ferried to school every morning. He also saw fishermen in *sampans* with their catch. Khoo decided to join the navy to see the world and to serve Singapore. By an accident of history, he served in the Malaysian Navy for 29 years and was the person responsible for the establishment of the Malaysian naval base at Lumut, Perak.

He studied at Outram Primary School and Raffles Institution from 1951 to 1955. He was an all-rounder and represented RI at athletics and swimming. He was also a prefect, Boy Scout, cadet and actor with *The Raffles Players*.

Khoo lived in Pulau Bukom, where his father was a petroleum analyst with Shell and one of its first Asian executives. He had intended to be a doctor and had turned down a Shell Scholarship in order to join the Navy. In 1956, he was one of the pioneering batch of nine from the Commonwealth who gained admission to the Britannia Royal Naval College, Dartsmouth, and in 1958, he graduated with the Queen's Commission. After serving 18 months with the Royal Navy in an aircraft carrier in the Mediterranean Sea, he was despatched to Cyprus to maintain order in the Civil War. "I saw action for four months and I inadvertently got involved in someone else's War. Meanwhile, the

Singapore government had handed over the Royal Navy to Malaya. So I was given away, together with all the small ships, buildings, stores and equipment. During the Indonesian Confrontation, I opened fire and sank an enemy vessel loaded with arms and ammunition."

He was posted to the Ministry of Defence as Naval Secretary to the Chief of Navy and played a key role in the design and construction of fast patrol boats and the refurbishment of the coastal minesweepers and the first frigate, *KV Hang Tuah.* He supervised its maiden voyage from Britain to the main naval base in Woodlands in 1964. Remembering the May 13 incident as a dark day for Malaysia, he recalled that he was in charge of patrolling the roads and feeding the people of Kampong Batu. The navy was called in to help. "It was frightening, because during a riot, people don't care who they shoot at."

The need to start a naval academy became evident in the early 1970s. New officers had to be trained to replace officers who were loaned by Commonwealth navies and to meet the Royal Malaysian Navy's expansion programmes. Training overseas was too expensive. The suitable location for a naval academy came in the form of an abandoned army camp in Sembawang. Khoo directed the major renovation work and transformed the camp into the official RMN training establishment in 1971.

When Singapore separated from Malaysia in 1963, it was vital that the Royal Malaysian Navy should be based on Malaysian shores. The search for a good location had started in 1960. Finally, Lumut in Perak was chosen as it was a natural harbour. It was established in 1979.

As Fleet Materials Commander, Khoo Tee Chuan oversaw the construction and development of the Malaysian Naval Base, transforming it from a sleepy hollow. He was also the first Commanding Officer of the Naval College, *KV Pelanduk,* in Lumut.

In 1984, after a distinguished career spanning 29 years, he retired. If it had not been for an accident of history, Khoo Tee Chuan would most probably have been Singapore's first Chief of Navy. Malaysia's gain is Singapore's loss.

Of Chemistry and Longevity

Kiang Ai Kim

Kiang Ai Kim is the first Singaporean Professor of Chemistry. In his lifetime, he has seen the evolution of the Raffles College to the University of Malaya in Singapore and, after two more evolutions, to the current National University of Singapore. Yet this unassuming 88-year-old professor would not have realised his ambition, if fate had not smiled kindly on him on two occasions. When the Japanese forces invaded Singapore, he was forced, at rifle-point, into a concentration camp in Jalan Besar. When he was interrogated, he gave his occupation as a laboratory assistant. Somehow, this did not impress his captors and he was released after two days. Later, a friend told him that he was reporting at the Kempetai Headquarters in Orchard Road because he had heard that young men would be given jobs. For some inexplicable reason, Kiang did not follow him. His friend, a Queen's Scholar in Botany, was never seen again.

Kiang studied in Raffles Institution from 1931 to 1934. As he could not afford to go abroad to study Medicine or Law, his teachers advised him to study Science, which was an entirely new subject. To Kiang, the local teaching staff were more understanding and concerned about their students while the expatriate teachers tended to be more aloof and unapproachable.

Kiang graduated from Raffles College, an institution whose primary role was to produce teachers for the growing number of schools which could not be filled by expatriates. Later, the local graduates were recruited into the Civil Service.

As Professor of Chemistry, he introduced new courses, which included Applied Chemistry, opening the doors for graduates to find employment in the industry. He also advocated the introduction of disciplines such as microbiology and food technology. He was personally involved in the planning and design of the University's Science Tower.

As an idealistic young man, Kiang was affected by the anti-colonial struggle and was a member of the Malayan Democratic Union. But he parted company with his friends to devote his energies to his first love — Chemistry. His work as a teacher and researcher has produced many outstanding graduates, who are now making significant contributions to the nation.

At eighty-eight and a great-grandfather, he is still spritely and mentally alert, as he nostalgically recalls his youth and adult life, with clarity and modesty. Once a chain-smoker, he has successfully kicked the habit. A former President of the Old Rafflesians' Association and the National University of Singapore Society, he is a staunch supporter of their activities. He is also a respected and popular figure with his former colleagues and students. He is also a keen gardener, calligrapher and trustee of the Society of the Physically Disabled.

Kiang's longevity can be attributed to his zest for life and to his lively interests in the world around him. In Raffles College, he participated in the corporate life of the campus. As a former student and professor, he takes an indulgent view of undergraduate pranks. "Ragging is part and parcel of university life, provided it's within limits. Some of the seniors who had ragged me later became my good friends." As the Master of Raffles Hall, he made periodic checks on the hostellites who hid firecrackers under their beds as ammunition for their assaults on Eusoff College, the women's hostel. He frequently had to intervene when the police or the fire brigade were summoned to Raffles Hall.

Chief of Armed Forces

Kirpa Ram Vij

Kirpa Ram Vij is Singapore's first Chief of Armed Forces and Brigadier-General. In his 45 years of distinguished public service in Singapore, he has served in the administrative service, the armed forces, foreign service and the national shipping line. He was engaged in action during Indonesia's policy of 'confrontation' against Malaysia and played a leading role in training Singapore's pioneering batch of national servicemen and in transforming our armed forces into the lynchpin of Singapore's national defence. He had intended to be a teacher but he proceeded to the university on the advice of his teacher, which changed the course of his life.

Kirpa Ram Vij was born in India in 1935. Following the partition of India, he found himself in a refugee camp in Pakistan. When he was eleven, he came to Singapore, and was over-aged when he entered Rangoon Road Primary and Victoria Afternoon School. He studied in Raffles Institution from 1953 to 1956 and was a school prefect and a quartermaster of the Cadet Corps. A keen actor, he was in several *Raffles Players* productions, including the role of John of Gaunt in *Richard II*. He also played rugby and hockey.

"My father was a petty trader. I was the eldest of eight children and had no great ambition. It was merely a question of survival. I intended to be a teacher to support the family. It was Mr Philip Liau who advised me to enrol in the university and that changed the course of my life." With the aid of a bursary, he graduated in Geography in 1960 from the then University of Malaya in Singapore. He was a student councillor and president of Raffles Hall. After his graduation, he served in the Land Office and Ministry of Finance. In 1960, he received the Sword of Honour when he was in the Singapore Voluntary Artillery. During the Indonesian Confrontation, he was mobilised as an Artillery Officer in the Malaysian Armed Forces. "We were in charge of the searchlight batteries and mortars in Johore. When the Indonesians came, we fired flares and guns. Looking back, it was fun." He was also mobilised during the racial riots in 1964.

In 1965, when Singapore attained Independence, he was seconded to the Singapore Armed Forces. He served with distinction, becoming the founding Director of the Singapore Armed Forces Training Institute and the Singapore Command and Staff College. He earned rapid promotions to Commander of the 3rd Singapore Infantry Brigade, Director of General Staff and Chief of Armed Forces. As Brigadier-General, he became the army's highest ranking officer.

He is proud of his contribution to Singapore's national service. "It is the best thing that could have happened to Singapore. We are a multiracial society and national service transcends ethnicity and economic status. After they were demobbed, our young men found immediate jobs as storekeepers, drivers and mechanics. It is also a cheap way to provide a deterrent force. Otherwise, it will be a drain of our financial resources."

After nine years in military service, Kirpa Ram found another niche — in the foreign service — when he was appointed Ambassador to Egypt with accreditations to Yugoslavia, Pakistan and Lebanon from 1975 to 1979. "It was like being thrown into the deep end of the pool, as I had no previous experience in diplomacy." Nevertheless, he proved equal to his task, while the various countries were undergoing crucial changes. His last government posting was as General Manager of Neptune Orient Lines, a position he held from 1981 to 1995.

Kirpa Ram had four successful careers in government service spanning 45 years in all. "I had four jobs, each one completely different from the other. My policy is that you should put your heart and soul into whatever you have been assigned. You can only do your best. In my case, it has turned out to be so. I have derived a lot of satisfaction and pride for what I have achieved. I happened to be in the right place and at the right time. My generation was lucky. No other generation will ever be placed again at such a vantage point."

Kirpa Ram Vij is too modest about his achievements. In Singapore's military history, his place is assured.

The Sky's the Limit

Koh Chai Hong

Koh Chai Hong has the unique distinction of being Singapore's first woman pilot in the Republic of Singapore Air Force. She is the highest-ranking woman officer in holding the rank of Lieutenant-Colonel at the age of 40. In a remarkable career spanning 27 years, she has held many important posts, including Squadron Leader and Chief Instructor of Fighter Pilots. She is also a former national water-skiing champion.

She studied at Tanjong Katong Girls Secondary School and at Raffles Institution, where she completed her 'A' levels. She was an outstanding athlete and won colours in the school's women's hockey team. In her career, where split-second decisions are vital, she jokingly recalls how she was occasionally late for school, missing the bus which took her from her home in Chai Chee to RI in Grange Road.

The young Chai Hong became interested in flying when she attended a career talk. "I never expected to make a career out of flying. Flying then was more of a hobby than a profession. "I just wanted to continue flying and I was fortunate and grateful that the air force allowed me to do so. I also had to overcome parental objections."

She joined the Junior Flying Club and earned her Wings in 1979. She became a Flying Instructor in 1981 and rapidly rose through the ranks, reaching the grade of Instructor of Instructors and Flight Commander. She is the first woman Squadron Commander in Singapore. She retired as Lieutenant-Colonel in 2005.

Koh frankly admits that her career has not been plain sailing, or should we say, plain flying. She had to overcome many prejudices, especially in the beginning. "It was very tough, being the first woman pilot breaking into a new domain which was essentially a male sanctum. I never thought of myself as being in a male-female situation. Rather, I tried to focus on my strength as a professional pilot and do the best I can. It has been a very fulfilling career."

It was a proud day for her when she participated in the fly-past in the 1995 National Day Parade. "I was co-piloting a *Hercules C130.* We waited for more than one hour in the air before we could zoom and thunder past the cheering crowd below. It was only a few seconds, but we had to rehearse several weeks for it."

Her only possible regret is that she did not become a fighter pilot. "When I graduated, I wanted to be the best pilot I can be. The best pilot goes to become a fighter. They had planned to put me there. Somehow, it did not happen. I topped all the Flying prizes. I was the best in Basic and Advanced Flying and also in Aerobatics. I also topped the Flight Instructor course. Nowadays, when I fail a trainee, he's demoralised, because I'm a woman." Equally at home in the air or at sea, she was a SEA Games medallist at water-skiing.

Koh Chai Hong is a pioneer in Singapore's military history. She has blazed an inspiring trail for other women to follow in her illustrious airborne career. She is an unsung heroine who has trained many RSAF pilots to protect and safeguard Singapore's territorial integrity and national security.

International Playwright

Stella Kon

Stella Kon *nee* Lim Sing Po, is one of Singapore's foremost playwrights. She achieved international fame with her play *Emily of Emerald Hill,* which has been staged in many cities throughout the world.

Stella is a true blue Rafflesian, having received her primary, secondary and pre-university education at Raffles Girls' School. Her tertiary education was at the University of Singapore where she graduated with an Honours degree in Philosophy. What is most surprising about her literary achievements is that she never read Literature in the university.

Her literary success is largely due to her parents. "My father, Lim Kok Ann, passed on to me an interest in Science and a love of Literature. He was a great reader and he liked reciting poetry. From him, I learned a sense of rhythm and developed a feeling for words. My mother, Rosie Seow, was an ardent and pioneering stage actress in the 1950s. From her, I learned a lot of stagecraft and sense of the theatre."

Her mother would proudly show her young daughter's writing to her friends and this greatly encouraged the budding writer. Stella was already writing plays, when she was a schoolgirl. She made a clean sweep at the triennial national play writing competition organised by the Ministry of Culture, by winning it in 1979, 1982 and 1985. Her prize-winning entry, *Emily of Emerald Hill,* was submitted in 1985. "They stopped running the competition after that. Probably they thought that I would keep on winning." However, *Emily* did not make its debut until many years later. "When it was finally publicly presented, I boasted that

I was Singapore's greatest never produced playwright, since I had won three top prizes and none of them had been produced at that point of time."

Emily was initially staged in Malaysia and then at the Singapore Arts Festival. Since then, this classic monodrama with a one character cast has fascinated audiences in Edinburgh, Sydney and Hawaii. It is staged virtually every year back home.

Emily of Emerald Hill has been adopted as a Peranakan icon, as the play revolves round its sole character, the *nonya*. *Emily* appeared at a time when Peranakan culture was on a rising wave and was the first play to depict the Peranakan character. It was not intended to focus primarily on its heritage as it is the story of a woman who clutches on to those she loves and in so doing, alienates them. "It was her lesson in later life that if you really love something, let it go. Then, it might come back to you."

Stella has written several short stories and two novels. *The Scholar and the Dragon* was published in 1985. It is about a Confucian boy who came to Singapore in 1910 and made his fortune. For this, she draws inspiration from her great-grandfather, Dr Lim Boon Keng. The work *Aston* won her the Singapore Literature Prize in 1995. It is about the search for a spiritual life in the context of this very materialistic city.

Stella does not keep to a strict regime when writing. She is more concerned with themes and that is why her plays and novels may take years to bear fruit. They are, however, worth waiting for.

Stella Kon belongs to the school of writers of the 50s and 60s who were concerned with nation building, and it is a theme which keeps recurring in all her works.

Stella Kon admits that it is a labour of love. "If you can sell 3,000 copies within the first six months, it is already considered a bestseller. The market is even smaller for poems and plays. Bookshops demand a 50 percent commission and prefer international writers. However, I'm cautiously optimistic for young writers provided they can receive more support in terms of sponsorship from corporations."

The Westernised Oriental Gentleman

Kwan Sai Kheong

Kwan Sai Kheong devoted his life to education. He was a brilliant all-rounder, being a mathematician, artist, violinist, inventor, linguist and Ambassador.

He was born in Malacca in 1920 and had his early education in Chinese, before coming to Singapore to study in Outram School and Raffles Institution. He joined the Raffles College in 1938 where he stayed in the Eu Tong Sen Hall with 100 other undergraduates from Malaya and Singapore. The hostellites had to observe total silence between 2 pm and 4 pm daily, because of the ongoing lectures and tutorials in the campus. Promptly at 4 pm everyday, they would be distracted by Kwan practising on his violin. His one-hour session would send his philistine friends running off to the playing field or to more remote parts of the campus.

After graduating with an Arts Diploma in 1941, he joined the OCBC, a rare appointment in those days, unless one had influential family connections. Obviously, Kwan was recruited because of his knowledge of Mandarin and Mathematics. He had the great opportunity of becoming a wealthy pioneering banker. He returned home only at night, because of the long banking hours and complained that he never saw the sun. His heart was not in it and he lasted only one year, primarily because he was not motivated by the pursuit of money. He opted for his first love — education. After the War, he joined the Education Service and taught in RI from 1947 to 1953. His students were often enthralled by his mathematical wizardry. When they failed to understand his lectures, he did not admonish them but would encourage them with his gentle, indulgent smile.

With the aid of a scholarship, he went to London to study Art and was made an Associate of the Royal College of Art in 1956. He was Vice-Principal of the Teachers' Training College from 1957 to 1960. He rose rapidly within the Service and was eventually appointed as the Permanent Secretary and Director of Education. In 1959, he obtained his BA Honours degree from London University.

Kwan represented Singapore with distinction in many international conferences, including UNESCO. He also served in the University Council, crowning his illustrious career by becoming the Vice-Chancellor of the University of Singapore in 1975, where he saw to the smooth transition of the University from Bukit Timah to Kent Ridge. He was awarded the Public Administration Gold Medal and the Meritorious Service Medal.

A true artist, his other passion was in painting in which he loved portraying the beauty of the female form. He was undoubtedly influenced by his training at the Royal College of Art. With his multifaceted talents, Kwan was popularly regarded by his friends and colleagues as a luminary and a genius. He was also an inventor and had patented several inventions.

Kwan Sai Kheong died in 1981, while he was the Ambassador to the Philippines. He was an exceptionally talented public servant who devoted his life to education. A Westernised Oriental Gentleman, he was in the words of Lee Kuan Yew's tribute to him, "a shrewd and philosophical man, though somewhat resigned to the wayward ways of many people in an imperfect world. He brought to his work, high imagination and striking powers of analysis, but his intellectual brilliance was tempered by his humility."

Chief of the Navy

Kwek Siew Jin

It was because Kwek Siew Jin did not like the army and was rejected by the air force that he was drafted into the navy. He commanded the Singapore Navy's first minesweeper on its maiden voyage from San Francisco to Singapore. After 27 years of distinguished service, he retired as Chief of the Navy with the rank of Rear-Admiral (Two-Star). On returning to civvy street, he presided over the SMRT Corporation Ltd and Singapore Power. He is currently the President of the National Council of Social Services and Chairman of the National Centre for Philanthropy and Volunteerism.

He studied at Serangoon Garden South Primary School and he did not know of the existence of RI, until he was tipped off by his friends. "When the PSLE results were announced, I found that I had been posted to RI. So a moment's decision led me on the path of discovery and learning which I had never even dreamt about and gave me the opportunity of studying in the premier school of Singapore." He studied at RI from 1963 to 1968, graduating in Electrical Engineering from the University of Singapore on a SAF Scholarship. He was also a graduate of the Harvard Advanced Management Program.

Siew Jin is philosophical about his achievements. "Some people believe in planning every step of their lives and try to keep closely to the chosen paths. However, I look on life as a series of opportunities that appear and disappear to be grasped as one wishes. There is not just one road in life. On looking back at how I came to be where I am today, I see a pattern of opportunities that took me from one part of my life to the next, unfolding without great forethought or planning."

He recalls how he could not afford to go to university, as his father had died when he was in Secondary 3. "I had to look for a job after my HSC. National service was beckoning. I thought that instead of spending three years in the army as a foot soldier, I could do better by signing up as a regular in the SAF for six years. I had always dreaded joining the army and having to crawl in the wet mud and dirt in a mosquito-infested jungle. So I decided the best course for me was to apply for the air force, as a pilot. I passed all the tests, except that my legs were not long enough to depress the pedals of the Hawker Hunter aircraft. To my great surprise and joy, I was inducted into the then Maritime Command as a midshipman officer cadet and sent to Australia for two years' training. On my return, I was commissioned as a 2nd Lieutenant, which was the beginning of my adventures in the Singapore Navy, which was to last 27 years — a journey which took me to many countries and where I met many people and which equipped me with many skills. Most important, it has allowed me to serve the nation in the critical area of defence capability of our fledging navy."

Every naval officer looks forward to his first command at sea. Kwek Siew Jin's opportunity came in 1975 when he commanded a minesweeper which the Maritime Command had purchased from the US Navy. "I attended courses in Mine Warfare and Mine Countermeasures. This was a new field of maritime warfare, particularly important because of the strategic importance of our sea lines of communications. When I saw my ship *The RSS Jupiter* for the first time in the San Francisco bay, I was filled with pride and joy. Even though she was as old as I was then, she looked every inch a naval ship, ready to tackle the rigours of a long ocean voyage and sail the width of the mighty Pacific Ocean and get home to form the nucleus of the new warfare capability of Singapore." The epic journey took 66 days and covered 13,000 kilometres, anchoring at Pearl Harbour, Guam and Subic Bay. Kwek and his pioneering, but inexperienced, crew had set a record for two small wooden vessels sailing halfway round the world.

Kwek Siew Jin retired as Chief of the Navy with the rank of Rear-Admiral (Two-Star), after 27 years of distinguished service during which he held various appointments in operations, logistics and manpower management. Now, on dry land, he prefers to travel by the MRT instead of driving his Mercedes. There should be a moral in this somewhere.

Founding Father

Lee Kuan Yew

Lee Kuan Yew is the founding father of independent Singapore. Born exactly 100 years after the founding of Raffles Institution, he is without a doubt the most eminent Rafflesian. In 1959, he became Singapore's first Prime Minister at the age of 36. For 31 years he ruled supreme, transforming Singapore from a Third World colonial entrepôt into a First World nation. He is *primus egalitus* among his Cabinet colleagues. He was appointed Senior Minister in 1991 and Minister Mentor in 2004.

Both Lee Kuan Yew's life and political career have been extensively researched and documented. He himself has written his memoirs *The Singapore Story* in two volumes. Governments elsewhere seek his advice on development issues and his views on a changing world, particularly the rise of Asia. The world media constantly clamours to interview him. Needless to say, his lifetime achievements extend far beyond the scope of what is etched in this profile.

Lee Kuan Yew is a fourth generation Chinese Singaporean, his great-grandfather having emigrated from Guangdong province in 1862 to Singapore at the age of 16. Lee Kuan Yew was born on 16 September 1923 at 92 Kampong Java Road. His father first worked as a storekeeper with Shell, and later at a jewellery shop. His parents gave him the name 'Kuan Yew', which means 'The light that shines far and wide'. He was educated at Telok Kurau Primary School and Raffles Institution, where he topped the Senior Cambridge Examinations in Singapore.

When asked about the chief influence of RI, he says, "Coming to RI from Telok Kurau English School, I found many bright students who did better than me. So I had to make a greater effort to get nearer the top. Admission to Raffles was on merit, regardless of a student's race, religion or social background. Hence, RI had students who were rich and were driven to school in cars, while large numbers took buses, or walked or cycled as I did. But for work and study, it was a level playing field for all."

Lee Kuan Yew achieved his mastery of the English language by listening carefully to the native speakers who taught him in RI in Junior and Senior Cambridge. They were an Englishman, a Scotsman and an Australian. He also read books written in good English, such as essays by Charles Lamb or Bacon, the plays of Shakespeare and selected poems and sonnets.

The young Lee proceeded to Raffles College, where he read English, Mathematics and Economics. His university education was interrupted by the Second World War and the Japanese Occupation (1942–1945). During the Occupation, he worked as an English language editor in the Information Department. He graduated with Double First in Law from Cambridge University in 1949 and a star for distinction in the final examination. Returning to Singapore, he joined the firm of Laycock and Ong before establishing his own practice, Lee and Lee, with his wife.

Lee Kuan Yew had read Law instead Medicine because he felt that he could fight for clients in court better than look after sick patients. "Law and Medicine were the only two professions in colonial Singapore where I could be self-employed, and not work for the government or some large British company."

In 1950, Lee Kuan Yew married Kwa Geok Choo. A Queen's Scholar, she was educated at Methodist Girls' School, RI, Raffles College and Girton College, Cambridge, where she holds the distinction of being the first Singaporean woman to graduate with First Class Honours in Law in 1949. They have two sons, Hsien Loong in 1952 and Hsien Yang in 1957, and a daughter, Wei Ling, in 1955.

Lee's wife, has been his lifelong partner both at home and at work where they had been partners in their law firm, Lee and Lee. In politics, his wife helps in correcting his transcripts and drafting his speeches. He says, "She knows my vocabulary, is familiar with my diction and makes my English clean and clear. Clarity is her professional skill as a draftsman, drafting agreements, contracts and wills."

In 1954, Lee Kuan Yew became a founder member of the People's Action Party, and in 1955, he was its Secretary-General when he contested the General Election in the Tanjong Pagar Constituency and became one of the three PAP Assemblymen. He has remained the representative of this Constituency since 1955. In 1959, he became the Prime Minister of self-governing Singapore when the PAP romped home with a spectacular victory, winning 43 of the 51 seats. His remark "The verdict of the people is a terrifying thing" is forever enshrined in Singapore's political vocabulary.

There were many highlights and memories in his political career, some of which have been described in his memoirs *The Singapore Story*. "Some of these were turning points where," as Lee says, "had things gone wrong, *The Singapore Story* would have ended differently." He names three of them:

"First, my meeting with Communist underground leader, Fang Chuang Pi, the Plen, who was in charge of the Singapore section of the Malayan Communist Party. In 1958, I was the leader of the Opposition in the Legislative Assembly and met a wanted Communist leader, the Plen, in secret. It was momentous because after meeting him, I understood how serious he was about his revolution. He had the pallid look of someone who has been in hiding, a fiercely determined face and bright piercing eyes. The lesson I took back was that unless we were equally determined and serious about our objective for a democratic, non-Communist society, we stood no chance against them.

Second, a radio broadcast I made during the 1964 riots on Prophet Mohamed's Birthday on 21st July. I realised how fragile inter-racial and inter-religious harmony was in Singapore, with racial and religious agitation. It led to bad feelings because of race and religion. It was a harrowing moment. Nobody listened to my appeals to stop killing. The riots had to be put down by force.

The third unforgettable occasion was when I met Tengku on Saturday, 7 August 1965. He told me separation was the only course left, because if Singapore stayed on in Malaysia, he could not stop the bloodbath. I tried to persuade him to carry on, with Singapore in Malaysia. He had already made up his mind. So it was separation from

Malaysia. It was a most painful decision. By agreeing, my colleagues and I let down thousands of Chinese, Indians and other Malaysians who had rallied to our cause in the Malaysian Solidarity Convention for a Malaysian Malaysia. Not a Malay Malaysia.

These were seminal moments. I cannot afford to regret. I made the best decision I could, with the knowledge I had at the time."

Lee is acknowledged as *primus egalitus* by his Cabinet colleagues. He says, "As the Prime Minister, I was younger than several of my colleagues in the Cabinet. However, I was the most prominent leader because I was the principal communicator. It was natural that I should be *primus inter-pares.* Whenever there was a public dispute over any important policy, I have to defend it and persuade people to support the policy."

Lee Kuan Yew would like to be remembered as having done his best, working with the people he had and the resources at his disposal. For Rafflesians and Singaporeans, he has this inspiring message: "The future is not pre-ordained. You can influence your future. Decide what you want to do with your life and try to make life better for all Singaporeans." He will always be remembered as the founding father of modern Singapore and the leader who took Singapore from the Third World to the First.

The Chinese Mandarin

Lee Siow Mong

Lee Siow Mong (seated in photo) held the rare distinction of being in the pioneering batch of civil servants in the Singapore Administrative Service. He was an internationally renowned authority on Chinese art and culture and also the driving force of the China Society. He was probably the last of the Chinese Scholar-Mandarins of Singapore.

Lee was born in Singapore in 1915 and acquired a classical Chinese education after his father sent him to China at the age of seven. At twelve, he returned to Singapore where he attended an English school. However, he continued his Chinese education under private tutors, learning calligraphy, seal carving and painting.

From Raffles Institution, he proceeded to Raffles College, where he graduated with a Science Diploma. He was a pioneering recruit when he entered the Straits Settlements Civil Service in 1937. He also studied Public Administration at Oxford.

Lee held several top posts, including those of Director and Permanent Secretary for Education, and General Manager of the Public Utilities Board. After his retirement, he was appointed by the Malaysian government as the General Manager of the Employees Provident Fund.

He was trilingual, proficient in Mandarin, Malay and English. He also lectured in the University of Malaya. He wrote three authoritative books on Chinese art and culture. His name became synonymous with the China Society, of which he was the President from the 1950s. The Society is devoted to the study and promotion of Chinese art and culture. Lee loved music and learned to play the Chinese harp, flute and fiddle. He mastered Chinese calligraphy, seal carving and brush painting, and collected jade and porcelain pieces. But he was no bookworm, for he also mastered the martial arts of the five Masters. His daughter, Lee Tzu Pheng, is a poet. His son, Tzu Yang, is Chairman of the Shell Companies of Singapore.

Lee Siow Mong's friends and colleagues regard him as a gentleman in the true sense of the word. Throughout his working life, he always followed his conscience. He was the typical civil servant but he was warm and friendly, and always forthcoming with advice to those who sought it from him.

Lee died in 1989 at the age of 75. He had devoted his life to the promotion of Chinese art and culture as one of the vital components of a multiracial society. Lee had always kept a low public profile. His valuable contribution to Singapore's cultural heritage was not immediately recognised until much later.

Of Mergers and Acquisitions

Lee Suet Fern

Lee Suet Fern is the founder and Senior Director of Stamford Law Corporation. Her firm was the first law corporation to be established under the Legal Profession Act of Singapore. Stamford Law is a corporate law firm focusing on mergers and acquisitions, corporate finance and capital markets related work. She has found her niche in this very specialised area of Law. She is also an advocate and benefactor of women's education.

Suet Fern's Malaysia-born father, Lim Chong Yah graduated from the then University of Malaya in Singapore with the aid of a Straits Settlements Scholarship. He was Professor of Economics at the University of Singapore and Chairman of the National Wages Council.

Suet Fern received her early schooling in Oxford, where her father obtained his doctorate and at Petaling Jaya, where he was a lecturer at the University of Malaya in Pantai Valley. She was educated at RGS (1971–1974). She was an ASEAN Scholar at the National Junior College (1975–1976). She graduated with a Double First Tripos in Law from Cambridge University in 1980.

She recalls the two main influences in her life. "My sense of motivation for the value of hard work and learning — a lot of that came from my father. The second phase came very much from RGS. That is why I'm such a staunch Rafflesian. RGS had a tremendous number of girls who were incredibly talented. There were some girls who had no money to buy school uniforms. I then felt that I had no excuse not to excel in my studies for I did not have to worry if there was enough food at home. There was also a tremendous sisterhood which all girls share. That was an important part of the RGS spirit which I still enjoy today."

A brilliant student, she was also a First Class Girl Guide, debater, actress and orator in English and Malay. She was a member of the victorious National Junior College team which won the national televised debates.

Suet Fern reveals that she realised her full potential at Cambridge. "I felt very challenged and very stretched intellectually. I was left very much to study on my own. There were very few lectures and tutorials. That actually worked very well for me. I enjoyed spending the whole day in the library and the opportunity to be challenged by teachers who were intellectually incredible."

Why did she choose to study Law instead of Economics like her father? "My father wanted a doctor and a lawyer in the family. As my younger brother had opted for Medicine, I obediently studied Law. I had little choice. It was a binary option," she jests.

Suet Fern reveals the ingenuity behind the selection of a name for her firm. "We were the first law corporation in Singapore. No one else dared take advantage of the new legislation. I didn't want to use my own name. Raffles was too common and you had to write in for permission to use it. I wanted a linkage to Singapore with a bit of subtlety." As its founder and Senior Director, she can be truly proud that her firm is a leader in a very specialised field. "We do domestic and cross border mergers and acquisitions. I discovered that the world of business fascinated me. We advise and ensure that businesses do not breach a whole myriad of laws and regulations. In this area, there are a lot of complex securities laws and regulations involved."

A champion and benefactor of girls' education, she generously donated $125,000 to her *alma mater.* "Many successful old boys give back to their schools. There aren't enough examples yet from old girls. I wanted to help create such a spirit, by leadership and example, with my donation. I specifically earmarked it for Science and Mathematics. Girls can also be immensely talented in these subjects. I had majored in Science. We need to create an environment where people regard an education for girls as important as that for boys."

Suet Fern successfully fulfils her role as a career woman, wife and mother. She is also candid in her views, as a member of the famous Lee family. "I love my family very dearly. I have been very lucky to have the support of a strong and secure husband in Hsien Yang and my three sons. Sometimes my work has to take priority. I also have fantastic in-laws. They are wonderful human beings who enjoy their children and their grandchildren."

In our interview, Lee Suet Fern comes across as a brilliant, dynamic and enterprising woman. She is charming and gracious, brimming with humility and her laughter is infectious. A visionary pioneer, she leads by example in the legal profession, in girls' education and in community service.

Paper Wizard

Leong Cheng Chit

Leong Cheng Chit is an internationally renowned origamist. Many of his designs have been published in journals of *origami* societies in Japan, USA and Europe. He is acclaimed not only for his immaculate folding, but also for his erudition in the great variety of his work, which ranges from mathematical models to sculptures.

Leong studied at Pearl's Hill Primary School and was at Raffles Institution from 1958 to 1963. He was a prefect and the school's high jump champion. He was a Scout and the assistant Scout Master as well as the art editor of *The Rafflesian*. A Colombo Plan Scholar, he graduated with a First Class Honours in Naval Architecture from the University of Glasgow. He was also a graduate of the International Senior Management Programme at Harvard University.

For 23 years, he worked in the Economic Development Board acquiring considerable experience in many areas of industrial development and investment promotion. He was the Senior Projects Officer and Centre Director of EDB with offices in London and Stockholm. He was also Head of European Operations of Engineering and Director of Industry. After leaving EDB, he held several directorships in the corporate world.

"I came from a humble background. My parents were simple folk, but they encouraged their children to study hard and to do well in school. My father was the first generation in Singapore and had a traditional Chinese upbringing. He was a commercial artist with an advertising company and I inherited my artistic talent from him. Opportunities for a career in Art were poor in those days. So I went on to study Engineering." When he was a primary schoolboy, his family lived in a hut which served as a grocery store. He learned how to calculate and to make the most efficient use of scraps of paper and newspaper to wrap the groceries. This experience nurtured his interest in *origami* in his adult life.

Origami is derived from two Japanese words: *ori*, which means 'folding' and *gami*, which means 'paper'. Simply, it is folding from a piece of paper, normally a square without cutting. Forty years ago, people folded traditional models, which included the crane, frog and paper boat. *Origami* took off in Japan in the 1960s, chiefly due to the efforts of one man, Yoshizawa, who formalised the traditional folding patterns and created new models of his own.

Leong Cheng Chit waxes lyrical when he explains how he fell in love with *origami*. "To the layman, *origami* is a Japanese craft providing a useful pastime for kids. To a serious *origami* enthusiast, it is an art form with a strong mathematical foundation. I had not known of the tremendous advances in *origami* when I took it up six years ago. I started from instructions in books and found that I could create new models. There are two directions of development in my *origami*. I experiment with curves, rather than straight fold. It is generally called 'tension folding'. The other direction is the more traditional style of folding, using straight fold. Many of my designs have been published in international *origami* journals."

Leong laments that only a handful of Singaporeans are creative folders. He advocates that *origami* can be taught as a subject in Art schools and as part of Industrial Design in polytechnics. He points to the permanent public sculptures and art works based on *origami* throughout the world. Among the creative folders are scientists and mathematicians who have produced beautiful and highly complex art pieces. Paper folding principles are now used in Architecture, Engineering and Molecular Biology.

Leong Cheng Chit believes that creativity and the arts should also be sustained by research and development, the same way they are lavished on the sciences and on economic development. He calls for greater government and corporate support and funding to invest in our promising local talents. Local works of art should be prominently displayed in our museums and libraries.

Rags to Riches

Lim Boon Keng

Lim Boon Keng's success story is the stuff of which every schoolboy's dreams are made of. At the age of 16, he was faced with the prospect of leaving school, but he became the first Singaporean Queen's Scholar. The Queen's Scholarship was a prestigious scholarship previously awarded only to the children of expatriates. Later, Lim Boon Keng used his wealth and influence for the benefit of education and the community. In the 1950s, he was affectionately known as 'The Grand Old Man of Singapore'.

His father, born in Penang, came from a second generation family in the Straits Settlements, but he was born in Singapore in 1869 and was admitted into Raffles Institution in 1879. His Principal was surprised by his knowledge of the English language and Literature which he had acquired from books borrowed from friends. At sixteen, when his father died, Lim nearly had to leave school. Luckily for him, his Principal, Mr R. W. Hullett persuaded his grandparents to let him continue his studies. He also found a benefactor in Mr Cheah Hong Lim.

In 1886, Lim Boon Keng became the first Chinese to be awarded the Queen's Scholarship. He was second to Song Ong Siang in the examinations, but Song was only awarded it the following year, because he was underage. Lim studied Medicine at Edinburgh University.

He founded Sincere Dispensary. He was a famous physician and a wealthy man, investing in property, rubber and tin. His old School Principal was never forgotten and he expressed his gratitude by naming the road next to his house 'Hullett Road'.

At twenty-six, he was appointed the first Chinese member of the Legislative Council of the Straits Settlements. He was awarded the OBE. He founded the Straits Chinese British Association and the Chinese Volunteer Force. Always conscious that the local Chinese should not lose their roots, he encouraged the English-speaking *babas* to study Mandarin. The queue was sported by men in those days and Lim led the queue-cutting campaign as the queue was the symbol of Manchu bondage. He also devoted his efforts to campaign against opium smoking.

Lim Boon Keng founded the Singapore Chinese Girls' School in 1899 on the grounds of his family home. Although this met with poor response from the Chinese community, he was undaunted and persevered in raising funds and rallying support. He was thus a pioneer in women's education.

At the request of Tan Kah Kee, Lim Boon Keng agreed to leave a life of comfort and achievement in Singapore to become the President of Amoy University. He remained in Amoy from 1921 until his return to Singapore in 1937. This was not a happy period of his life as his advocacy of Confucianism clashed with the Chinese intellectuals of the May 4th movement.

In 1942, when the Japanese authorities set up the Overseas Chinese Association, Lim was forced to lead the organisation and mobilise the collection of $50 million from the Chinese in Singapore and Malaya. He also acted as the intermediary between the Japanese masters and their subjects and was credited with saving many lives.

Lim Boon Keng died in 1957 at the age of 73. A nationalist, reformer, educator, philanthropist and community leader, he used his wealth and influence to ameliorate the plight of the ordinary people. In the hallowed school hall of RI, he heads the select company of Queen's Scholars.

Nationalist and Patriot

Lim Bo Seng

Lim Bo Seng was a wealthy young man when Singapore fell to the Japanese forces in 1942. He abandoned his life of luxury and ease to become a guerilla and freedom fighter. He sacrificed his life for his country and was only thirty-five when he died.

Lim was born in Fujian, China in 1909. He came to Singapore when he was sixteen. His father owned a brick factory and was the contractor who built Victoria Memorial Hall and the Goodwood Park Hotel. Realising the value of an English education, he enrolled Bo Seng at the Junior Cambridge Class in Raffles Institution. Bo Seng had studied in a Chinese school in Amoy and English was his second language but his teachers were impressed by his keen intellect and his hunger for books and English literature.

Lim was tall, thin and pale. There was no indication that he would develop into a master of intrigue and espionage. He furthured his studies at Hong Kong University, but they were interrupted by his father's untimely death.

On returning to Singapore, he introduced new ideas into his father's business and prospered. He was an entrepreneur, manufacturing bricks and biscuits. He also traded in flour, sugar and coffee beans. He was also a keen gardener and photographer. He played tennis and bred goldfish. Lim Bo Seng was in his twenties and basking in luxury and comfort. But he always fought for justice and fair play. He had gone to Kuala Trengganu to organise a strike by the workers. His leadership qualities were recognised by the British authorities. Instead of arresting him for damaging their economic interests, they cultivated him as their undercover agent to monitor the Japanese underground activities in Singapore.

His clandestine activities paled in comparison to his later heroic exploits. In 1935, the Japanese occupied Manchuria, followed by a full scale invasion of China. He was prominent in the China Relief Fund. In December 1941, when the Japanese bombed Singapore, he led the 10,000 defence force in maintaining essential services. With Singapore's imminent fall, he was advised by the governor to flee Singapore and continue his resistance efforts elsewhere. Lim had only a few moments to bid farewell to his wife and seven children. The Japanese soldiers went to his house and took away his male relatives.

Lim and his men escaped in a motor boat and were picked up by a British steamer. The captain revealed that he was from Force 136 and that they were training local guerillas to resist the Japanese. Lim was promoted to Lieutenant-Colonel and went to Chungking. With the support of the Kuomintang government, he recruited Malayan exiles to enlist in the Force. The guerillas disrupted communication lines, in preparation for British amphibious landings. They were the nucleus of the Malayan People's Anti-Japanese Army.

In Ipoh, Lim led a cavalier double life, winning the trust of the Japanese officers and reporting vital information to the resistance movement. The end came when he was betrayed by one of his comrades, a triple agent who worked for the British, French and Japanese. Lim was arrested and tortured in the Batu Gajah prison. He died with his lips sealed on 27 March 1944, bravely refusing to divulge incriminating information about Force 136. In his last letter to his wife from prison, he wrote, "I fully realise the risks involved. But, once the job was started, it must be pushed to a successful end. My duty and honour would not permit me to look back. Every day, tens of thousands are dying for their countries." His diary was recovered after his death. It contained one moving entry. It was addressed to his wife and children. "Do not grieve for me. You should be proud of me, for what I have done."

A memorial service was held on the steps of the City Hall on 13 January 1946. A procession of armoured cars, British and local survivors of Force 136 escorted his body to a state burial at MacRitchie Reservoir, where a memorial was erected. Another monument, a pagoda was erected in 1950 at the Esplanade, with contributions from 50,000 Singaporeans. An oil painting of Major-General Lim Bo Seng by the renowned artist Liu Kang adorns the walls of the SAFTI Headquarters. It is a present from his children, in loving memory of their famous father.

Lim Bo Seng made the ultimate sacrifice expected of a soldier. He gave his life for freedom and for national honour. His patriotism and courage will always remain a source of inspiration for many generations. Lim Bo Seng was every inch a citizen soldier.

The *Chatek* Queen

Carmee Lim

Carmee Lim *nee* Carmee Lee has the triple distinction of being a former student, teacher and Principal of Raffles Girls' School. Under her leadership, RGS moved to Anderson Road and became an independent school and also held the distinction of being the first school to introduce computers.

Carmee Lim first received her primary education in a Chinese school, before proceeding to RGS. As a young student, she played netball and *chatek,* the feather-shuttle, during recess. "I was the *chatek* queen because I could use both legs. We were caught by the very strict expatriate Principal who dismissed it as something most unladylike."

From Raffles Institution, she proceeded to the University of Singapore. After her graduation, she became the senior science teacher at Crescent Girls' School and in 1969, she taught in RGS. Later, she became the Principal of Woodsville Secondary School, and after that, a senior inspector of schools.

Carmee assumed the prestigious office of RGS Principal in 1988 and was the fifth Singaporean to do so. She gave new insights into education, such as "The mind is not a vessel to be filled, but a fire to be ignited. Learning is no longer a sedentary activity. Learning is tied to emotion, because emotion drives learning. You must get your students interested, so that they can find relationship and attachment, so that they will learn. When I was teaching Physics, I introduced them to Newton's Law of Motion by telling them to kick a football."

Carmee is proud that RGS was the first Singapore school to use computers. She introduced cyber learning into the curriculum so that her students would be acquainted with information technology.

She played a leading role in the design and planning of the new RGS premises in Anderson Road, which was opened in 1993 and was also the person responsible for the successful transformation of RGS into an independent school. She had embarked on making RGS into a school for the future to keep pace with the new learning environment. Thus, the Cyber Learning Centre bears her name. Carmee has also nurtured the development of speech and drama, music and dance as well as community involvement programmes, believing that a caring and sharing school environment builds character. "Our school motto is 'Daughters of a Better Age' but, we must not rest on our laurels. We must dare to be active creators for a better age for the future generations."

She is married to Lim Jit Poh, a Rafflesian and Science graduate of the National University of Singapore, who has held top positions in the Singapore education service. Carmee sings in the choral society and plays the jazz drums and composes songs for children. She is a qualified aerobics instructor and the President of Singapore Gymnastics. For this, she draws her inspiration from her schooldays as a *chatek* queen. She is the Chairman of the Parent's Advisory Group for the Internet (PAGi) which is concerned with Internet safety. Under her leadership, PAGi has reached out to more than 90,000 children, youth, parents and volunteers.

Carmee Lim has received several awards for her contribution to science education. Her former colleagues and students speak affectionately of "the Principal with the ready smile and a scarf round her neck, brimming with ideas, passion, dynamism and boundless energy."

Reach for the Sky

Lim Chin Beng

Lim Chin Beng is popularly known as 'Mr SIA' He started as an administrative trainee, became a Managing Director and culminated his 30-year career with SIA as its Deputy Chairman. He is a pioneer in civil aviation, having nurtured and transformed the Singapore International Airlines (SIA) into one of the world's leading carriers. He is a pioneer in civil aviation.

Lim studied at St Xavier's Institution and the Penang Free School. When his parents moved to Singapore, he was admitted to Raffles Institution where he excelled in basketball because of his height. It also enabled him to play the double bass. While he was an undergraduate, playing with a band earned him a monthly income of $200. An Economics graduate of the then University of Malaya in Singapore, he worked as an administrative officer in the Treasury for four years.

In 1960, he joined the Malayan Airways as an administrative trainee and opted for a lower salary. "I was more interested in a different office culture, where there were fewer regulations and bureaucracy. I was keen to see the results of my work immediately. It also coincided with the Malayan Airways policy of Malayanisation. So the moral of the story is — don't worry about the short term, even if you get a salary cut. The long term outlook is more important. You should follow your own interests."

SIA was established in 1972. "I was fortunate enough to be the most senior Singaporean around and I was appointed its first Managing Director." But he had no illusions about the daunting tasks that lay ahead, as SIA flew into uncharted territory. "Right from the start, our policy was to have a product of international standing. I got hold of the famous French couturier, Pierre Balmain, to design the uniform for our stewardesses. This *sarong kebaya* uniform has stood the test of time for the past 33 years and is the most recognisable airline uniform anywhere in the world. However, the image of the Singapore Girl had provoked resistance from Western countries. They branded us as sexist."

In our 90-minute interview in his Singapore Press Holdings office, Lim Chin Beng vividly recalls the early days. His modest and unassuming demeanour belies his passionate commitment to make SIA succeed. In the early seventies, SIA took the crucial decision of acquiring Boeing 747s to equip itself for long haul flights. "There were other aircrafts that were less expensive, similar in size and less risky. It was the biggest risk that we took." The rest is history. In the 1980s, SIA faced new challenges, including rising oil prices and double-digit wage increases. It underwent cost-cutting and under-manning. "Our determination and strategy paid off. Today, SIA has the most productive work force of all the world's airlines."

Being a newcomer, SIA also had to fight against the protectionism and landing rights imposed by Western countries. "It was a very tough struggle, but the main thing is service. Many people have asked me why SIA is so successful. My answer is that it is the special quality of the Singapore Girl. In addition to the Asian culture of courtesy, we have an advantage over our regional rivals, because our girls can speak good English and can communicate better with the international passengers." He dismisses any suggestion that he was the brains behind SIA's transformation. Voted 'The Businessman for 1986' he attributes his achievements to the dedication of his staff. "It is all a matter of timing. Everything in life depends on timing. You have to think big. If you think small, you will not succeed so well. So it's a question of being bold, perhaps being foolhardy, and to have faith in your product."

In his distinguished career, he has served as the Chairman of the Singapore Tourism Board, as Member of the Public Service Commission, and as Ambassador to Japan. He was the Chief Negotiator of the Singapore–Japan Free Trade Agreement. He served as Chairman of the Singapore Press Holdings. He was also the founding Chairman of ValuAir, a budget airline carrier. He is the Co-Chairman of the Japan–Singapore Symposium.

Lim Chin Beng is a visionary for nurturing and guiding our national flagship to achieve world status. A pioneer in the field of civil aviation, he has dared to dream the impossible dream, so that Singapore International Airlines can reach for the sky and fly all over the world — the pride and joy of all Singaporeans.

A Nuts and Bolts Minister

Lim Hng Kiang

Lim Hng Kiang dealt with explosives when he was a soldier. As a young boy, he witnessed the nearby Bukit Ho Swee fire and the Hock Lee Bus riots. He was confronted with the most hazardous situation when he was the Health Minister during the SARS outbreak. In his 12 years of distinguished service, as CEO of the Housing and Development Board, Deputy Secretary and Minister for National Development, he engineered the upgrading of HDB flats and the blueprint for the revised Concept Plan for Singapore.

Hng Kiang was born in 1954. His father was a staff sergeant in the police force and his mother a housewife. They lived in a SIT flat in Alexandra Road and had six children. "In the surrounding areas, there were *kampongs* and Bukit Ho Swee squatters. In Redhill, farmers reared pigs and poultry." He attended Alexandra Estate Primary and was one of the three students who were admitted to RI (1967–1972). "At Raffles, we had a sense of history. It had a great tradition of public service. The school had many nooks and crannies where we could take cover with friends. The attic was reputed to be haunted. Our teachers provided the motivation and the scope for the students to grow and nourish. RI gave us the opportunity to develop our organisational and leadership qualities. We took on responsibilities beyond our age. That is the quintessence of the RI experience."

As a student librarian, Hng Kiang developed a love for books and reading. He was in the pioneering batch of the Air Cadet Corps, rising to the rank of Lieutenant. "My greatest joy was to be given a two-hour lesson to fly a Cessna 172. It was great fun, building up the Corps from scratch. I also spent three weeks in the USA as part of the Air Cadet Exchange. It was my first trip overseas. I stayed with a farming family in Oregon. I had a culture shock, when they brought me to a supermarket and carted the provisions they had bought in three trolleys."

A brilliant student, he was a President's Scholar and also a SAF Scholar. He graduated with a First Class Honours degree in Engineering from Christ College, Cambridge in 1976. He also obtained his Masters from Harvard's Kennedy School.

He served in the Singapore Armed Forces for nine years, holding Command and Staff appointments. He produced an instructional film on explosives. "Not many young officers have the chance to blow up the entire range of explosives in the SAF inventory." He also participated in demolishing the gun emplacement bunkers in Tanah Merah to make way for the new Changi airport. "We spent the whole day out on the beach enjoying the sun and sea and we sang, but really all the while doing very serious work." As Head of Air Planning, he reviewed the role of the air force as an important strategic component of Singapore's defence capabilities.

Lim Hng Kiang was in the Ministry of National Development for 12 years, including five years as its Minister, during which time he was responsible for all the different stages of policy development, implementation and modification. These included the review of the Concept Plan for Singapore and the upgrading of HDB flats. "We also had the ethnic policy to ensure that we did not create racial enclaves again." Hng Kiang has often referred to himself as a 'nuts and bolts' man who is reliable and who gets things done.

He was elected as a Member of Parliament for the Tanjong Pagar GRC in 1991 and for the West Coast GRC in 1997.

He was the Health Minister during the 2003 SARS outbreak. "It was the longest four months of my life. We were monitoring the developments as they unfolded. SARS was completely new. There was a tremendous fear of the unknown and mass panic. If it had not been for our health workers, our health system would have broken down. As the Minister, you realise that you are just part of a huge team in which everybody plays a part, right down to the hospital attendant."

Lim Hng Kiang is always modest and conscientious about his responsibilities. How does he view his present job? "The Ministry of Trade and Industry is a very exciting Ministry. It covers so many economic sectors, including manufacturing and tourism. It has a very huge impact on the well-being of Singapore."

Lim Hng Kiang has an inspiring message. "What makes us distinctive is that what we have has been created by our forefathers and by ourselves. As long as we are creative and innovative, there is no reason why we cannot continue this success story."

The Girl Who Guides

Lim Hsiu Mei

Lim Hsiu Mei reached the pinnacle of her career after 37 years of distinguished service in the elite Administrative Service of Singapore. She has played an invaluable guiding role in the Girl Guides movement, her *alma mater*, as well as in public and community service. She is also one of the pioneers in hospice care development. She was the first Chairperson on the Board of Governors when RGS became an independent school.

She received her entire education at RGS and proceeded to RI (1957–1958). In 1962, she graduated with a degree in History from the University of Singapore. She hails from a family of Rafflesians, which comprise her three sisters and one brother, Lim Kuang Hui, a septuagenarian, who still has the 'Boy Scout' in him. An ophthalmologist, he is passionate about Harriers running and mountaineering, looking at ice when not looking at eyes.

As a schoolgirl, Hsiu Mei had her fair share of thrills and spills. "My mother called me a tomboy. I went camping, pitching tents under the stars in Singapore, Johore and the Philippines, and going hiking with the Boy Scouts. I also got into trouble with the school authorities. Once, a classmate I was carrying accidentally slipped and fell. I was wrongly accused by the Principal of being the ring-leader of bullying my classmate. We also played tricks on the Latin teacher by throwing stink bombs in class and blaming the foul smell on the chickens reared by the school servants." She remembered her 1956 class as being the first in RGS to achieve 100 percent passes for the Senior Cambridge Examinations.

She has remained a Girl Guide since her schooldays. 'Once a Guide, always a Guide' is a motto she believes in. She has been through the entire ranks of the Movement, holding positions, such as Brownie Leader, the Lieutenant of a Guide and Ranger Company, President of the Trefoil Guild, Deputy Chief Commissioner, Vice-President and Adviser. For her contribution, she was accorded the highest Guide awards, the 'Palm Leaf Gold' and the 'Orchid'. "I have seen the Guide movement grow out of its colonial shell to keep pace with Singapore's political development," she says. Under her dynamic leadership, a new constitution was established and the Guide uniform was redesigned. New proficiency badges were introduced, including those for Musketry and Foot Drill and also for Crime and Drug Prevention.

She has also loyally kept her ties with her *alma mater*, the Raffles family of schools. She was among the pioneer batch of Executive Committee members of the primary school. She chaired the secondary school Advisory Board and guided the development of RGS into an independent school in 1991. She holds the unique distinction of being the first Chairperson of its Board of Governors. "We can recruit the best teachers and attract talented students. We have flexibility in student admission, charging of fees, syllabus and fund-raising. RGS has produced excellent results since it became independent."

Lim Hsiu Mei retired in 1999 after 37 years of distinguished public service. In 1975, she was the first woman to be appointed to the superscale Deputy Secretary grade of the Administrative Service. She was also the first Non-Education Officer to head the National Institute of Education. She had also served in the Ministry of Interior and Defence — where she was dubbed 'That Bold Girl', the Public Works Department as well as the Ministries of Finance, Education, Social Affairs and Community Development. As recognition for her contribution to public service, she was awarded the Public Administration Gold Medal.

These days she lends her guiding hand to the Hospice Care Association as its Honorary Secretary, and also the Dover Park Hospice. "A hospice is not a death house. It's also not about dying, but living. It means accepting death as an inevitable part of life, calmly and peacefully. It ensures quality of life, even to the last day."

In her life and in her career, Lim Hsiu Mei has scored many firsts. She is truly a trailblazing Guide.

Have Wings, Will Fly

Lim Kim Choon

Lim Kim Choon is the Chief of the Republic of Singapore Air Force with the rank of Major-General. He is a qualified F16 and A4 fighter pilot who has held many top appointments in the RSAF. In his distinguished 24-year career, he served as Head of Air Intelligence Department, as well as Head of Air Operations Department. He was also the Commander of Tengah Air Base and Chief of Air Staff. He became Chief of Air Force in 2001 at the age of 44.

Lim Kim Choon received his secondary education at RI and completed his 'A' levels in 1976. With the aid of a SAF Scholarship, he graduated in Production Engineering from the University of Loughborough. He obtained his Masters in Management from the Massachusetts Institute of Technology, and for his advanced military training, he attended the prestigious Air Command and Staff Course in the USA.

He did not originally aspire to a career in the air force. "I did not come from a well-to-do family. All I wanted was to go to university and have a good career. It has certainly been an eventful and rewarding career, all thanks to the Defence Ministry. I had no real aspirations to fly, but since I was physically fit for the job, I accepted the challenge and soon fell in love with it. I started with the A4 and subsequently, with the F16 fighter jet. There is no greater thrill than to get out of the office and fly. When you are in the air, there are no distractions. You are free and focused to kill your adversary. It is a great getaway."

What Lim Kim Choon values most is the training of the mind and the opening of new worlds. He recalls how, as an undergraduate at

Loughborough, he had the opportunity to see things from a different perspective. "It was my first time overseas and the first time that I felt lonely. But independence came quickly and I did not have to worry about finances. So I could concentrate on my studies, make friends, and learn about other cultures. It was an invaluable learning lesson and a useful preparation for my working life."

He describes his 24-year career in the air force as "invigorating." He was among the pioneers who set up the SAF Joint Intelligence Directorate, working closely together with colleagues from the army and navy.

It was at MIT that he was exposed to the private sector since many of his classmates were from the business world. "I learned a lot about how corporations are run and tried to bring those insights back to the military world."

He considers the highlight of his career to be in 1997, when he took command of the Tengah Air Base. "As Commander, you are intellectually tested at staff level and emotionally tested at commander level. I had to deal with policies and implement them, which were real challenges. Earning the respect of over 2,000 personnel was not easy. In the military, you don't get respect because of your rank, but through professionalism and understanding of the issues which your men are worried about. As Commander, I learned to sympathise and empathise — to strategise with my mind, but to implement with my heart."

Lim Kim Choon stresses that the top priority for the RSAF is the need to adjust the cultural mindset of the men to better anticipate and to deal with the unexpected, especially after 9/11. The air force has to adjust to the new global realities and security environment, and also to regional threats like piracy and smuggling. "RSAF must be prepared to face asymmetric threats. Our objectives remain largely unchanged, that is, to ensure that RSAF is a capable and operationally ready air force to defend Singapore."

Lim Kim Choon started his career as a fighter pilot, popularly known as 'Rocky'. Now, as its Major-General, he is eminently qualified to lead the RSAF in safeguarding Singapore's air space and national territorial integrity.

Of Medicine and Chess

Lim Kok Ann

The name of Lim Kok Ann is synonymous with the game of chess in Singapore. In his lifetime, he had coached and inspired many National Grand Masters. As they grappled with him across the chessboard, his protégés would have known that their mentor was a Queen's Scholar and a Professor of Virology. They were soon put at ease by the unassuming ways and infectious sense of humour of the bespectacled professor.

As a young boy, Kok Ann stayed with his grandfather, Dr Lim Boon Keng, who was the President of Amoy University in Fujian. He was fascinated by the numerous junks and ships which plied the harbour and often dreamt of distant lands and places.

He was educated at the ACS. He was admitted into the RI Queen's Scholarship Class of 1936. His classmates included Kwa Geok Choo, later to become Mrs Lee Kuan Yew and E. W. Barker. Like every westernised oriental gentleman, he also tried his hand at cricket. It was after he was painfully struck above his right eye by a ball from the school's fast bowler while keeping wicket, that he decided to settle for the less dangerous game — chess. He was awarded the Queen's Scholarship and studied Medicine in Edinburgh University. In 1958, Lim Kok Ann won international fame when he was the first virologist to isolate the influenza virus of the Asian flu.

His love for chess nearly cost him his life. He had gone down to London to play chess but, at that time, German air raids were so intensive that he returned to Edinburgh. The following week he learned that the bookshop where he was to play had been destroyed by a German bomb.

Lim was the first Champion when the Singapore Chess Tournament was inaugurated in 1946. He devoted his life to grooming and coaching the post-War generation of National Grand Masters. He was very generous and donated innumerable books, sets and clocks. He also sponsored young chessmen to compete in national and international tournaments. He was the Life President of the Singapore Chess Federation and as well as the Secretary-General of the World Chess Federation, FIDE. He also coached and inspired blind chessmen, blindfolding himself and taking on six of them simultaneously. "When I was in Edinburgh, we experienced frequent blackouts, because of the German air raids. Often, we were guided by a blind colleague from the library to the hostel. Since then, I always have great respect and faith in the ability of blind people."

Although Lim Kok Ann's other interests included bridge, billiards and *mahjong,* his first love was chess. He was a legend in his lifetime and present and future generations of chessmen will always remember, with affection and gratitude, his pioneering service to the game of chess.

An Extraordinary Soldier

Lim Neo Chian

During his career, Lim Neo Chian has worn many hats, distinguishing himself in the army, industry and tourism. He was Chief of Army holding the exalted rank of Major-General. As Chief Executive and Chairman of the Jurong Town Corporation, he was a key mover in the development of the wafer fabrication parks and the establishment of Jurong Island as a world-class chemical hub. Now, as Deputy Chairman and Chief Executive of the Singapore Tourism Board, he is charged with the responsibility of developing Singapore's tourism sector into a key economic driver for Singapore.

Lim Neo Chian pays tribute to his father and to his *alma mater* for his success in adult life. "My father was the manager of a rattan shop in Boat Quay. We lived in a two-room SIT flat in St Michael's Road and I was the second of seven children. My father had the added responsibility of looking after us when my mother died of breast cancer when I was 10 years old. He impressed upon us the importance of studying hard as this was the path to a better life. He gave us prize money whenever we did well in school and I really appreciated the hard life he must have led. I attended Towner Primary School. One day, as we were travelling in a bus when it passed Bras Basah Road, my father pointed out RI to me and said that he hoped that I would study there. Thus, he was overjoyed when I was admitted to Raffles in 1966. I realised that there were many students who were smarter than me. In RI, you competed against some of the best students in Singapore and you got better in the process. I am quite certain that my life would have been very different if I had not gone to RI."

In 1975, Lim Neo Chian graduated with a First Class Honours degree in Engineering from Sheffield University. He also attended the Development Management and Advance Management programmes at Harvard. He did not plan to have a career in the army. "I took up the SAF Scholarship because I wanted to go overseas to study. I also received a monthly salary of $1,500, which was important for supplementing my family income. Career development in the SAF was developed to a high level of sophistication, with few equals even in the private sector. Young officers were given responsibilities quite unmatched elsewhere. At the age of 32, I was appointed Assistant Chief of the General Staff in charge of the planning functions of the army. I was in charge of $800 million worth of capital expenditure for weapons procurement, camp construction and IT development." He served in key command and staff positions, including Commander of the 3rd Singapore Infantry Regiment and Chief of Army with the rank of Major-General.

Lim Neo Chian returned to civvy street in 1995 and had to adjust to his transition to civilian life. "There were moments when I asked myself whether it was worth it, but it was worth the effort. Very few people have the chance to take this path. I was lucky to be one of the very few." In his tenure at the Jurong Town Corporation, he was the driving force in inculcating a customer-focused culture. He was a key mover in several major initiatives, including the development of the wafer fabrication parks and the transformation of Jurong Island into a world-class chemical hub. As Chief Executive of the Suzhou Industrial Park, he actively promoted international investments. "I had spent three good years of my life there and have come to appreciate Chinese history, culture and people much more as a result."

As Deputy Chairman and Chief Executive of the Singapore Tourism Board, he was confronted by the nightmare scenario of the SARS outbreak in March 2003. "One hundred and fifty thousand people were dependent on the tourism industry. Changi Airport, hotels, shops and restaurants were empty. We needed to contain or reduce the impact of SARS on the industry and to work out a recovery plan. Much credit should go to the Health Ministry. We launched several campaigns. It was one moment in history when everyone worked as a team to solve a national crisis."

Under his visionary leadership, *Tourism 2015*, a strategic blueprint, was launched to underpin Singapore's position as a destination of choice and as a powerful exchange capital to attract visitors, businesses and talents globally. "We hope that the tourism industry will grow from 8 to 17 million visitors and from $10 to $30 billion tourism receipts. The government has set up a $2 billion tourism development fund and will proceed with the development of two integrated resorts in Singapore."

Descending the Ivory Tower

Lim Pin

Lim Pin ran a campus of 1,600 lecturers and 30,000 undergraduates. He is the first to be conferred the title of University Professor by the NUS for his visionary academic leadership.

He was born in Penang and came to Singapore when he was still a baby. His father was a Chinese School Principal. His parents inculcated in him certain Asian values. He attended a Chinese school, before switching to Geylang English Primary and RI. "My father had the foresight to see that if we stick to Chinese alone, things would be tough. My life would have taken a different route. I could have ended up as a radical or a prosperous merchant."

In his NUH office, we share memories of our schooldays punctuated by his frequent laughter. Lim Pin was born in 1936. In RI, he was a brilliant scholar, always topping his classes. He was a Queen's Scholar and Head Prefect. "On my first day in RI, I was overawed by the great reputation and tradition of the school. On the wall were the names of Queen's Scholars and Head Prefects. They had set the benchmark. They were the role models for inspiring us, at that impressionable age." Lim Pin aspired to be like them. But he did not know that by the time he graduated from RI in 1956, he would have joined the select company of famous Rafflesians.

"Scouting had taught me self-reliance and character. I went on a 16-mile overnight hike, pitching up a tent, cooking my own food and crossing the Jurong River. These adventures are etched in my memory. The Queen's Scholarship was a big leg up for me. My parents would not have been able to send me to Cambridge." He also showed his mettle as a schoolboy. His classmate had contracted tuberculosis of the spine and had to leave school for a long treatment. Nevertheless, he studied privately and requested that he be entered as a RI candidate for the Cambridge Examinations. But he was rejected by the expatriate Principal. Lim Pin succeeded in convincing the Principal to change his mind.

He also spearheaded the conversion of RI into the first independent school in Singapore in 1990. In retrospect, it was a good decision. It gave the school greater autonomy. The Principal could have more flexibility with the curriculum, the admission of students and fund-raising. RI also introduced the boarding school system.

He graduated from Cambridge in Medicine, where he also obtained his doctorate. He was attached to the Faculty of Medicine for 15 years, first as lecturer and then as Head of Department in 1979. He was the Deputy Vice-Chancellor, before his appointment as Vice-Chancellor of the National University of Singapore in 1981.

He remained its chief executive for 19 years, nurturing and developing the university through its formative years. NUS is now ranked among the top 20 universities in the world. "When I became the Vice-Chancellor, it was mainly a teaching institution, with hardly any research. I decided that if we were to make any impact, we needed a high profile in quality research. It also coincided with the transforming of the Singapore economy into a more high technology science-based economy."

The Institute of System Science was established in 1981. It marked the beginning of the university's first thrust into research and collaboration with industrial partners. They ranged from Data Storage to Molecular and Cell Biology. The NUS was internationally linked to Universitas 21. Cross-faculty modules were also introduced.

A $50 million Cultural Centre was built to enrich the cultural life of the campus and to encourage the students to express their artistic talents.

Lim Pin believes in foreign talent. "Singapore is so small. We do not have a critical mass, especially in research. Foreigners come here with their different sets of values and they also bring with them, good and fresh ideas."

He is the first to be conferred the title of 'University Professor', after 19 years as the Vice-Chancellor. He has gone back to his first love, Medicine, and specialises in endocrinology.

What is his philosophy of life? "I always believe that we should give ourselves the best opportunity to grow to the limits of our capability. We are all born with a set of potential abilities. Unless you are in the right environment to nurture and to grow, you will be lost. Not only for the person, but also for society."

First Woman Permanent Secretary

Lim Soo Hoon

Lim Soo Hoon has the unique distinction of being Singapore's first woman Permanent Secretary. After 18 years in the administrative service, she has reached the top of her career and is a role model for women who aspire to succeed in the public service.

She studied at Fowlie Primary School, which is no longer in existence. Her secondary education, from 1971 to 1974, was at Raffles Girls' School, where she was a prefect and also patrol leader in the 12th Girl Guides Company. She also excelled in sports and athletics.

Soo Hoon attributes her success in her career to her student days in the premier school for girls. "I learned about leadership and responsibility through my involvement as Patrol Leader of the 12th Company of the Girl Guides and as a school prefect. Those of us who had to play such leadership roles were very aware of our responsibilities and our influence on the young ones. I brought away with me the particular point that respect is earned through what we do and what position we hold. I learned about focus and discipline, and most important of all, team work and team spirit through athletics. We trained hard because we wanted to excel, not because we were pressured to." She recalls with pride that she was a member of the victorious RGS 4×100 metres relay team in the National Schools Meet. Its record time had stood for 20 years.

She is also grateful to RGS for her character development. "We were young and impressionable. There were certain values which the school and our teachers stood for. If they had not been there to mould and guide us, we would probably not be what we are today. RGS imbued us with values that last. Some values are taught and felt directly. But more often than not, we learned them directly through the experiences we shared and the activities we were involved in. We had students from different segments of society. Some of them had to be very mindful about their budget and family situation."

She still maintains close ties with her class. "We meet five or six times a year to celebrate our birthdays. Our friendship has matured over time. From giggling schoolgirls to grown women with giggling children of our own, we shared and are still sharing, our joys, our trials and tribulations all through our 29 years of close and warm friendships. We are there for each other during the darkest hours of our growing years and we are there during the brightest too. We still giggle a lot and we never fail to remember the good times — the hilarious moments we had, especially at the expense of our teachers, whom we still keep in touch with." In 1975, Soo Hoon proceeded to Raffles Institution to do her 'A' levels. She had been fascinated whenever her two brothers yearned about the school's scholastic and sporting achievements, and she was immersed in the school's great tradition and Rafflesian spirit.

In 1981, she graduated in Economics from the National University of Singapore. She also holds a Masters degree in Public Administration. In 1981, she began her career and has since served in various Ministries, including Communications, Labour and Community Development. She was also the Registrar of Vehicles and the Dean of the Civil Service College. In 1999, after 18 years in the Administrative Service, she was appointed Permanent Secretary in the Ministry of Community Development and Sports. She admits that being the first woman to hold a top post has been a humbling experience. "It was pressurising at first. It was also embarrassing and perplexing at times when people asked if it was tokenism."

In 2007, Lim Soo Hoon was named the 'Woman of the Year'; not just for her achievements in her career, but also for her devotion to her son who was battling against cancer. She wrote a book about her experience, entitled *Sam: A Mother's Journey of Faith.*

Lim Soo Hoon is an inspiring example of a woman with a successful career and a happy family. Today's generation of young women can learn much from the advice of this illustrious trailblazer. "Have confidence in yourself and make sure you stay close to your family, as they are your vital support in whatever you want to do."

From Clerk to Chief Minister

Lim Yew Hock

Lim Yew Hock was not born great. By his own admission, he did not achieve greatness. When he became Singapore's second Chief Minister, he had greatness thrust upon him.

He was born in 1914. He wanted to be a lawyer and his father had planned to send him to England to study Law, but his ambition was abruptly dashed by his father's untimely death when he was preparing for his Cambridge Examinations in Raffles Institution. At the age of 17, he had to support his widowed mother and his younger siblings. He gave private tuition and started his working life as a clerk in a British commercial firm, with a monthly salary of $25. His ability to master shorthand impressed his employers and he was promoted to stenographer and also, as private secretary to the manager.

Lim became a trade unionist, when he was employed as the General Secretary of the Clerical and Administrative Workers Union. His diligence and hard work paid off, when he was elected as the President of the Trade Union Congress. His rapid rise attracted the attention of the colonial authorities. He was appointed as a Nominated Member of the Legislative Council. However, this did not silence him and he was an outspoken critic of the repressive labour law.

With his experience as a trade unionist and as a legislator, it was only a matter of time before he gravitated into Party politics. In 1955, Lim was elected into the Legislative Assembly as the Labour Front candidate for the Havelock Constituency. He became the Deputy Chief

Minister, and also the Minister for Labour and Social Welfare, in the Labour Front Coalition Government.

Lim Yew Hock became Singapore's second Chief Minister in 1956. He succeeded David Marshall who resigned, following the failure of the Constitutional talks. He resumed negotiations with the British, paving the way for Singapore's internal self-government. He also granted Singapore citizenship to many of the disenfranchised Chinese immigrants. In the 1959 General Election, the People's Action Party won 43 of the 51 seats in the Legislative Assembly and Lim found himself on the Opposition bench. He retired from politics in 1963 when the Singapore People's Alliance did not win a single seat.

A close friend and ally of Tengku Abdul Rahman, he was appointed as Malaysia's High Commissioner to Australia. Later, he was Special Assistant to the President of the Islamic Development Bank in Saudi Arabia.

In his short memoirs entitled *Reflections* he wrote, "I have always been humble, irrespective of my position in life. I found that there is no true greatness in greatness itself, but there is truly greatness in humility. Lim Yew Hock was not great when he was Chief Minister in Singapore, but Chief Minister Lim Yew Hock was great, when he remained humble, in his relationship with his fellow men."

Lim Yew Hock was in politics for 15 years. His three years as Chief Minister were brief but important years. He paved the way for Singapore's internal self-government. He graciously stood aside for the PAP to assume power in 1959.

NCAR Astrophysicist

Low Boon Chye

Low Boon Chye is the Senior Scientist and Director of the National Centre for Atmospheric Research (NCAR) High Altitude Observatory at Boulder in Colorado, USA. He belongs to the select company of research scientists who specialise in studying the atmosphere and the sun. As a young man, he had to decide whether to be a shipbuilder or a space scientist.

Low studied first at Bartley Secondary School and then at Raffles Institution from 1964 to 1965. "I established a special bond with my classmates. I remember a sense of adventure, with discovery of something new each day at Raffles. Growing up to adulthood in the 60s in Singapore was a unique experience during the great social, economic and political changes of the time. I majored in Mathematics at King's College, but discovered that I liked solving equations rather than constructing ideas, which is what occupies modern Mathematics. That motivated me to leave Mathematics for Theoretical Physics." In 1972, he graduated from the University of Chicago with a doctorate in Magneto-Hydrodynamics by researching the fluid behaviour of plasma applied to the solar atmosphere.

Since he did not plan to live in the USA, Low and his wife returned to Singapore in 1975 to take charge of a family-owned small shipyard in Jurong. "My parents were entrepreneurs in the barge, tugboat, transport and shipyard business. I was not happy professionally, so I returned to the USA in 1979 with no job prospects. The scientific profession is very competitive but thanks to Prof Eugene M. Parker, I have never looked back. He is the man who predicted theoretically that the space of the sun out to the space between the planets is not vacuum, but is filled with a supersonic plasma. Modern space science began with Prof Parker's work and the space age." Six months later, I found my first job and was back to active research, settling into my present position in the High Altitude Observatory. Hence, my introduction to plasma physics and its application to the solar atmosphere. Astronomy is about phenomena. Astrophysics is about the physical principles operating in astronomical phenomena."

Low was also a Senior Research Associate with the National Aeronautical and Space Agency. His scholarly publications run into volumes and he is frequently engaged in lecture tours. "I opted for full-time research. I am still doing original work in theoretical Magneto-Hydrodynamics in the general area of solar influence on the earth and near space. An attractive feature of my work is my contact with many post-doctoral fellows who have come to work with me over the years. I am occasionally called upon to handle observatory leadership work."

Low Boon Chye, NCAR specialist in solar-terrestrial physics, is a world famous astrophysicist. This starry-eyed space scientist perpetually keeps company with a host of heavenly bodies. Although he is literally up in the clouds, his feet are firmly planted on the ground. He is modest about his achievements and shares his life's experience. "Find out how good you can be and where your talents are. Find out about yourself as a person and understand yourself, not in isolation, but in relation to the people and society around you. Information is what keeps us free, but is quite distinct from judgment and conviction, based on it. All the act is nothing without imagination and actual experience of life as it comes."

First Chief Minister

David Marshall

David Saul Marshall was a legend in his lifetime. When he became Singapore's first Chief Minister, he was already a famous criminal lawyer. At seventy, he began his diplomatic career as Singapore's Ambassador to France.

He was a Sephardi Jew of Iraqi ancestry. From St Andrew's School, he proceeded to Raffles Institution to study Science. He and his friends experienced racial insults from the expatriate staff and in one debate during which he likened the arguments of an expatriate teacher to 'the arguments of a cunning fox', he was immediately stripped of his prefect's badge. Marshall was a brilliant student and he wanted to study Medicine, but a bout of tuberculosis dashed his hopes and he had to leave for Switzerland for treatment. On returning to Singapore, he took on many jobs and used his savings to study Law in England. Through sheer determination, he passed his Law examinations in 18 months.

He was a Private in the Volunteer Corps and was taken prisoner by the Japanese and laboured in the coal mines of Hokkaido. Miraculously, he survived to keep his tryst with destiny. In April 1955, Marshall became Singapore's first Chief Minister, heading the Labour Front coalition government in the partially-elected Legislative Assembly. He was in office for only 15 months. After the Constitutional Talks collapsed, he resigned in disgust and declared that the British had offered only '*Tiga Suku Merdeka*'. Although his tenure of office was short, multilingualism, the Legal Aid Bureau and the Central Provident Fund bear testimony to his political legacy. "They were the most sustained ordeal of my life — not even excluding my prisoner-of-war days. But, they have been most rewarding." He was in Tengku Abdul Rahman's team for the historic Baling talks with Chin Peng.

He pioneered the lunchtime rally under the 'apple tree' at Empress Place. Clad in his famous bush jacket, he mesmerised his audiences with his brilliant oratory. Marshall did not completely disappear from the political scene. He founded the Worker's Party in 1957 and won the Anson by-election in 1961, although he was unsuccessful in the General Election of 1963.

In 1978 and at the age of 70, he was appointed as Singapore's Ambassador to France, where he was to perform his duties with dignity and aplomb for the next 15 years.

Marshall's brief tenure in office was a memorable time for Singaporeans. He was the man of the hour and he had led the people to throw off the shackles of the colonial yoke. He had kindled their yearning for freedom. He was flamboyant, temperamental, idealistic and politically naive. But he never wavered in his passion and commitment. He was a nationalist who fervently believed in multiracialism. Although he was from 'the minority of the minorities', David Marshall will always be remembered as Singapore's first Chief Minister.

Pioneer in Preventive Medicine

Ernest Steven Monteiro

Ernest Steven Monteiro was a pioneer in Preventive Medicine. He led the fight against poliomyelitis and beriberi in the 1950s, a period when Singapore was plagued by many diseases.

He was born in 1904 and attended St Anthony's Boys' School before proceeding to Raffles Institution. At the King Edward VII College of Medicine, he crowned his academic brilliance by winning many medals. In 1929, he began his medical career as a government doctor at the Tan Tock Seng Hospital. In 1939, he was awarded a Queen's Scholarship. He became a Member of the Royal College of Physicians in 1947. In 1948, he had the distinction of being the first Singaporean to occupy the Chair of Medicine. He was also the Dean of the Medical Faculty.

Monteiro was interested in the field of Preventive Medicine. The 1950s was a time when Singapore was plagued by numerous infectious diseases, resulting from poor living conditions, malnutrition and poverty. He introduced the use of vaccines, especially the Salk vaccine, on a mass scale, to protect children and adults from poliomyelitis. He also played a leading role in eradicating beriberi with Vitamin B1. His timely intervention and treatment saved many lives. His other contributions to medical advancement included the elimination of diptheria in children.

In the university, he was highly respected for his teaching and research. He was popular with his colleagues and students and as Dean of the Medical Faculty. He was affectionately known as 'Monty'. A dedicated academic, he was a modest and soft-spoken man, who occasionally enjoyed a game of *mahjong*.

In 1956, Monteiro was made a Fellow of the Royal College of Physicians. He was also a Pro-Chancellor of the University of Singapore. His academic papers were published in internationally renowned journals and he wrote three authoritative books. In recognition of his illustrious career, he was awarded the title of Knight Commander of the British Empire and a Fellow of the Royal Society for the Promotion of Health in 1972.

After retirement from his distinguished academic career, he was appointed Ambassador to Cambodia in 1965 and Ambassador to the USA in 1968.

Monteiro made his mark in the field of Preventive Medicine, being responsible for eradicating the two major infectious diseases which plagued Singapore in the early 1950s. He fought cardiac beriberi with Vitamin B1, and poliomyelitis with the Salk and Sabin vaccines. An excellent physician and clinician, he applied his vast experience and training in his diagnosis. This is quite remarkable since all this took place during an era when X-rays and laboratory facilities were in their infancy. His medical legacy is inspiring and profound. Ernest Steven Monteiro has indeed earned a permanent place in Singapore's medical and diplomatic history.

A Persian in Malacca Street

Mohamed Javad Namazie

Mohamed Javad Namazie was a Persian who originally practised law in Malacca Street. A Legislative Councillor, he was a pioneer in participatory politics in colonial Singapore. He had a distinguished record of public and community service, and was a highly respected leader of the Muslim Community. A gentleman and a gentle man, he never compromised on his principles.

Namazie was born in India in 1907. He came to Singapore at the age of six. His ancestors were traders and they ventured as far as Egypt, Iraq, India and China. He studied at the Convent of the Holy Infant Jesus and RI. He was a good student at RI and completed his Senior Cambridge Examinations at 15 years of age. The Principal advised his father to send him to England for further studies. At fifteen, he was too young to enter university, so he spent a year at Herne Bay College in Kent before going on to Oxford (Queen's College) where he completed his Law studies. He obtained an LLB and a Bachelor of Civil Law (BCL).

He was admitted to the Straits Settlements Bar in 1931 and in 1933, established the firm of Mallal and Namazie with its premises at Malacca Street. It was one of the pioneering local firms, in a colony of 100 Lawyers. At the age of 23, he became the trustee of his father's estate, which had considerable assets in property and rubber plantations. With the imminent fall of Singapore, he left for India, where he met with Tan Cheng Lock whom he knew earlier. The Namazies were helpful to Tan's family in finding accommodation in Bangalore where they lived during the War.

Namazie was elected to the Legislative Council in 1947 and he was appointed to the Executive Council, a post which he held for a few years. He supported the introduction of the Rent Control Act and the Income Tax Act. This was contrary to the interests of his own family, which owned substantial property. It was one of the many decisions which singled him out as a champion of the underdog and the disadvantaged.

He was a member of the Muslim Advisory Board (as was his father), and later on was appointed to the Majlis Ugama Islam and was a member for many years. He was one of the principal architects of the Administration of Muslim Law Act (AMLA).

Namazie played a crucial role in defusing communal tension, during the Maria Hertogh riots of 1951. Together with the Chief Kathi, and the Governor's Information Officer, G. G. Thomson, they drove through the mob, for a radio broadcast to calm the people. Namazie had even advised Thomson to wear a *songkok*.

Namazie was also instrumental in the establishment of the Darul Ihsan orphanage for girls. He was President of the Muslimin Trust Fund Association (MTFA) for many years. The MTFA administered the orphanages for boys and girls, amongst other things. His legacy can also be seen in the Maulana Mohamed Ali Mosque which is situated in the basement of the UOB Building in Raffles Place. The Muslim League's premises had stood in the way of the bank's expansion plans. Namazie succeeded in convincing the bank that Muslims should have a central place of worship, in the heart of the city.

It was said that Namazie was invited to be a member of the Tanglin Club and thus, his principles were put to the test. He politely declined the offer since he was an Asian and the Tanglin Club at that time excluded Asians from its membership.

A Rotarian, he passionately supported and contributed to community service. He was appointed to several boards and committees: the War Damage Commission, the Singapore Polytechnic, the Singapore Telephone Board, amongst others. He also served on the University of Malaya Appeals Committee. In 1966, Namazie was appointed as a member of the Constitutional Commission on Minority Rights. He was conferred the CBE, as well as other national awards. He was a great believer in education especially in the *madrasahs*, where he felt children should not only be taught religion but also scientific and technical subjects, which would be more helpful to them when they seek employment in the job market.

Namazie was a scholarly man who genuinely loved reading and books. His library included the English classics, Persian literature, Persian scripts and a set of the Encyclopaedia of Islam.

He was highly regarded by other lawyers for his honesty and integrity. He was a lightly built man, wore glasses and spotted a moustache. Friends often jokingly dubbed him as Groucho Marx. However, his quizzical smiling face belied his strength of character and his dedication to justice and fair play.

Mohamed Javad Namazie was a humanitarian and a family man. He had six children and they have inherited his passion for scholarship and community service. Two of his children were lawyers, Farideh (deceased) and Mirza. Incidentally, Farideh also went to RI for her pre-university studies. Hashim, who now lives in England, is an accountant. Manijeh is a retired librarian. Wahideh and Safiyeh were Arts graduates.

Mohamed Javad Namazie passed away in 1993 at the age of 86.

Veteran Educator

Noel Evelyn Norris

Noel Evelyn Norris has the triple distinction of being a former student, teacher and Principal of Raffles Girls' School. A veteran educator, she is also noted for her contribution to the community, drama, the Girl Guides movement and animal welfare.

From RGS, she proceeded to Raffles College. After her graduation, she began her teaching career with a monthly salary of $110 at the Bukit Panjang School. She was a teacher in RGS until 1956 when she became the Principal of Crescent Girls' School. She returned to RGS as the Principal in 1961 and retired in 1976. After her retirement, she taught at the School for Retarded Children.

"There were only ten of us in Raffles College. The professors allowed us to skip lectures, so that we could play bridge. The losers paid for potato chips." As a teacher, Norris was a first class narrator who seldom used textbooks. As a Principal, she was a dynamic leader who assumed her role with efficiency and total dedication and ensured that RGS kept pace with the many changes in the new national education policy. She was the first Principal to recruit male teachers in the school's sports programme. She also made it compulsory for all pupils to study both Science and Arts subjects. A firm believer in an all-round education and leadership training, she avidly encouraged extra-curricular activities, games, clubs and societies.

Norris was the person behind the scenes of the *Raffles Players* productions in her indispensable role as make-up and costume artist. With her reassuring presence and encouraging words, she ensured that the boys and girls did not suffer from stage fright. She also sewed the

Shakespearean costumes for the annual productions of the Singapore Teachers Union.

She started the 2nd Singapore Girl Guides Company. Norris also stressed the importance of personal grooming, character and moral values. She instilled in her students, the appreciation of nature and the ecology. Leading by example and not afraid to soil her hands, she was often seen doing the gardening and pulling out weeds together with the girls. The slogan 'Reduce, Re-use and Recycle' became her trade mark. According to her, nothing should go to waste. She also served in the Women's Auxiliary Corps of the People's Defence Force.

Norris looks back with pride on her 16 years as the Principal of RGS, when it became the top-ranking girls' school in Singapore. "It's the thrill of seeing the many successes of the girls, academically, culturally and in the ECA. The joy of receiving thanks from families and of having ex-pupils and teachers, who are now my personal friends and who I can rely on in times of need in my old age."

Her students remember her with affection and gratitude. They have happy memories of how she had moulded their character, by her sincerity, integrity and dedication. Today, many of them hold high positions in both the public and private sectors and much of the credit should go to Noel Evelyn Norris.

Mr Speaker

George Oehlers

G. E. N. Oehlers, or 'Geno' as he was popularly known to his friends, was a hockey legend. He also presided over the Singapore Legislative Assembly and the Industrial Court in Malaysia. With his stature and height, he strode like a Colossus among the Eurasian community.

Oehlers was born in 1908. His grandfather was the captain of a Danish ship who had decided to settle in Singapore. Oehlers was educated at Raffles Girls' School, St Andrew's School and Raffles Institution, where he excelled in hockey, cricket, soccer and volleyball. He was also the school's Head Prefect.

He read Law at Gray's Inn and was admitted to the Straits Settlements Bar in 1931 and established his own law firm. From 1933 to 1941, he served as a Municipal Commissioner, and from 1947 to 1954 as a Nominated City Councillor. In 1955, he was appointed the first Speaker of the Legislative Assembly. Then when Singapore attained self-government in 1955, he became the first elected Speaker of the Assembly.

Oehlers was an imposing figure in his Speaker's wig and robes. With his height and regal bearing, he looked every inch the Speaker. With his excellent grasp of parliamentary procedure, he imprinted his own stamp on his office and was highly respected by Members from both sides of the House. His task was not made any easier by the introduction of multilingualism in the Assembly, where members could speak in any of the four languages, namely Chinese, Malay, Tamil and English. His tenure of office also coincided with the advent of Singapore's two most brilliant orators — David Marshall and Lee

Kuan Yew. Their fiery exchanges often had the whole House as well as the public gallery enthralled. But Speaker Oehlers always presided over these debates with exemplary decorum, dignity and impartiality.

In 1965, he was appointed as the President of the Malaysian Industrial Court. Under his guidance, the Court was transformed into a respected national institution. He earned the trust and confidence of both his employers and employees, and was highly regarded as a man who believed in justice and fair play by all who knew him.

Oehlers was the inspirational captain of the Singapore hockey team for many years and in later years, was the *tour de force* of the Singapore Hockey Association. He was also the President of the Singapore Recreation Club. In the Eurasian community, he was its dominant figure and role model.

Oehlers died in 1968 at the age of 60. He had been awarded the OBE in 1953 and a knighthood in 1968. An unassuming man with a gentle disposition and a ready smile, he was unspoilt by success and treated his fellowmen with unfailing courtesy. His loyalty to his *alma mater* was firmly sealed when he held the office of President of the ORA for many years.

A True Blue Rafflesian

Mae Noleen Oehlers

Mae Noleen Oehlers holds the honour of being the first Singaporean to head Raffles Girls' School, a post previously reserved for British expatriates. She was the only woman to hold a super-scale post in the teaching service. In her 29 years of association with her *alma mater*, she had the triple distinction of having been a student, teacher and Principal of RGS. She was an excellent administrator, noted for her thoroughness and ability to organise.

Born in 1916, she was admitted to RGS as a pupil at the age of six. She studied there from 1922 to 1930 and remembered the school's big move in 1928 from the junction of Bras Basah and North Bridge Road to Queen Street. She attended Raffles College, where she earned an Arts Diploma.

Miss Oehlers always referred to RGS as her second home, one in which she had spent many happy years. She was an excellent Geography teacher and an Assistant Mistress and served under several expatriate principals for 15 years. She was responsible for the school's excellent results in the Senior Cambridge Examinations in the 1950s. From 1952 to 1956, she was Senior Geography Assistant during which time she organised the Geography Department. Miss Oehlers was a strict disciplinarian and students were always afraid to come unprepared for lessons. She had a fiery temper and her scoldings were unforgettable. But, she was effective, disciplining pupils to study Geography systematically from basic concepts to their application. At different times, she had taken on the responsibility of a netball and hockey convenor. Her brother, George, was a hockey legend. She was also interested in orchids and games. During the War years, she had worked in the Economics Department of the Colonial Office in London. After the War, she went back to RGS and resumed her teaching post.

Miss Oehlers assumed the exalted post of Principal of RGS on 8 November 1957, after having served in Cedar Girls' School for less than a year. Under her leadership, there were significant changes. She was responsible for the separation of the secondary school from the primary school and oversaw the subsequent move of the secondary school to its new premises in 1959. She also took a keen interest in fostering music appreciation and introduced morning and afternoon sessions. In 1961, she retired for health reasons.

To her friends and colleagues, Miss Oehlers was a friendly, warm-hearted, outspoken and kind lady, well-educated and refined, with a quiet sense of humour. She was very particular about the way pupils looked and school assemblies were occasions when she would emphasise the importance of good character. On her departure in 1961, she outlined what she considered to be good qualities — honesty, courtesy, and charity.

A true blue Rafflesian, Mae Noleen Oehlers is someone who epitomises perfectly the school motto *'Filiae Melioris Aevi'*.

Pioneer of Pantai Valley

Mohamed Taib bin Osman

Mohamed Taib bin Osman was the second Malaysian Vice-Chancellor of the University of Malaya in Pantai Valley, which was founded in 1961. The university had only four faculties — Arts, Science, Engineering and Agriculture — and was inadequately equipped to meet the developmental needs of a newly independent nation. Taib Osman joined it at its birth and witnessed its transformation into a national university producing competent and skilled graduates in various fields of endeavour. He retired as its Vice-Chancellor after 34 years of distinguished academic service. He created a precedent by promoting 30 academics to professors in order to avert a brain drain into the private sector. He was directly responsible for the establishment of the Faculty of Computer Science and Technology as well as the Academy of Islamic Studies and Malay Studies.

Taib Osman was born in Singapore in 1934. His father was Headmaster of Kota Rajah Malay School, the premier Malay school in Singapore. Taib first studied in this school, then Rangoon Road Primary, and finally Raffles Institution (1949–1954). He was a prefect, King's Scout and troop leader of the 30th Raffles Troop. "My most unforgettable memories were when we journeyed by train to play rugby against several Malayan schools. We, the urban boys, were clobbered, mauled and trounced by the sons of rubber tappers and paddy farmers."

He graduated from the then University of Malaya in Singapore and obtained his Masters from the University of Malaya in Kuala Lumpur.

In 1967, he received his doctorate from the University of Indiana. He joined the Department of Malay Studies as a tutor in 1961, and retired as its Vice-Chancellor in 1994, after 34 years in academia. For his outstanding contribution to university education, he was conferred an honorary DLitt and made an Emeritus Professor.

Taib Osman has played a key role in the various stages of the University of Malaya's growth and development. The Centre for Science Foundation was established to enable the rural population to receive higher education. It catered for the school leavers and conducted pre-Matriculation programmes for university entry. The Language Centre popularised and taught the national language to the students and staff in preparation for the medium of instruction to be converted to Malay eventually. It also conducted special English courses to meet various practical skills posed by economic globalisation. The university was faced with the political cry of nationalism to forge an identity for the new nation and the use of English as a second language. The Graduate Studies Centre was also established for postgraduate research.

Taib Osman introduced significant changes when he was the Vice-Chancellor. "The system of promotion to professorship had all along been dictated by the Civil Service system. This meant that only a few could reach the top rank. I promoted 30 academics to professors, which had never been done before. Another problem was the brain drain as there was always the attraction of better prospects in the private sector. The hardest thing was to achieve a balance. Promotion should not to be at the expense of academic standards. During my time at the helm, as IT was very dominant, I raised the Computer Centre to faculty level. My role as Vice-Chancellor was to provide leadership, and at the same time, not to lose sight of national and social responsibilities."

Taib Osman is proud that the University of Malaya is the oldest university in Malaysia. "In the spirit of friendly competition, it is possible for other universities to excel in their respective fields. Age goes with reputation. However, this university should not falter from the right path that it has been following, which is providing credible tertiary education for students, continually embarking on research and demanding high academic standards from its staff."

Taib Osman is a staunch advocate of university autonomy. "People at the university should be like a beacon in the community, showing good qualities as human beings and having independent and rational thinking." His place in the history of Malaysian university education is assured. As a pioneer of Pantai Valley, he has witnessed the transformation of the University of Malaya from a place carved out of secondary jungle and *lalang* inhabited by mosquitoes into a prominent institution of learning.

World Bank Specialist

Indra Padmanathan

Indra Padmanathan was the first Malaysian medical doctor to serve as a Public Health specialist with the World Bank. She achieved this prestigious international recognition for her pioneering work in Public Health Medicine in Malaysia and Sri Lanka. Her training manual in Health Systems research is extensively used worldwide, while her World Bank publication on how to make childbearing safer is internationally acclaimed.

Indra received her primary and secondary education at RGS and furthered her Post-School Certificate studies at RI (1953–1954). The foundations laid in Raffles enabled her to obtain the highest grades and win the prestigious University Entrance Scholarship to study Medicine at the UMS. She graduated in 1960, having received several academic honours during her school and university education. Her father was Mr Velauthar Ambiavagar, the first Singaporean Principal of RI. Indra and her two brothers are doctors. "I did not think that our parents had much influence on our decisions. Each of us made the decision for reasons of our own. Also, my father tried to discourage my determination to become a doctor because he thought that it would be too hard a life for a girl. Our parents taught us by their own example, rather than by preaching to us. We learned the glory of working hard and how to enjoy our work. We learned how not to give up, when faced with obstacles and not to expect favours from anyone. We find real pleasure in doing our work well. Certainly, we did not expect to become rich."

Indra married Padmanathan, a dental surgeon, and moved to Malaysia in 1961. She became a pioneer in the field of Public Health

Medicine in Malaysia and made several key contributions, notably the establishment of national programmes on health systems research and on quality assurance in health care, which have been internationally recognised as outstanding success stories. She was also responsible for upgrading and professionalising the Malaysian Health Inspectors programme.

"My work as a doctor was spent largely with very poor people, either in rural villages or urban slums. I used to walk through muddy lanes and rice fields to reach their houses. Once, I delivered a baby in a dark, wooden hut and needed to get water from a nearby well. I was at a loss on how to do it on a rickety old bed. I learned that the mother chose to have her baby at home because there was no one to look after her other children, and her husband was in the field all day. Within a few hours, she herself would be cooking for her family, while breastfeeding her newborn. I had to show her how to keep herself and the newborn free of infection and build her strength under those difficult conditions."

Indra has published a large number of academic papers and training manuals in her field of expertise. Her training manual on Health Systems Research has been translated into Spanish, French, Chinese and Vietnamese, and continues to be used in several countries in Asia and Africa. In recognition for her work in developing countries, she became the first Malaysian medical doctor to be recruited as a Public Health specialist by the World Bank in Washington, which recruits personnel through a competitive worldwide selection process. Among her contributions is a World Bank publication which analyses how Malaysia and Sri Lanka have been successful in making childbearing safer and in reducing deaths from childbirth.

Although she is an internationally renowned Public Health specialist, Indra Padmanathan is modest about her achievements. Nevertheless, she must certainly derive some quiet satisfaction and pride knowing that because of her pioneering efforts, countless thousands in Asia and Africa can now enjoy a better life, thanks to improved public health facilities.

Enigmatic Academic and Diplomat

Pang Eng Fong

Pang Eng Fong is an academic and a diplomat with a difference. As someone who performs both his tasks very seriously, he also has his funny side. As an academic, he challenges his students to reach their limits. As an Ambassador, he is never seen without his haversack. Thus, he is both a contrarian and a conformist rolled into one, who is not afraid to do the unusual or take the unconventional route.

He studied at Pearl's Hill Primary and at RI from 1958 to 1963. In 1967, he graduated from the University of Singapore, and in 1971, obtained his doctorate from the University of Illinois. He assumed the position of Director of the Economic Research Centre at the National University of Singapore before becoming an Associate Professor in the Business Faculty. He was also a visiting professor to the Universities of Michigan and Columbia. He has served as Ambassador to Seoul, Brussels and London. He is the Practice Professor of Management at the Singapore Management University and the Director of the Wee Kim Wee Centre, as well as the Lee Kong Chian Scholars Programme.

Prof Pang is heartened by the more vibrant and diverse educational landscape. "This is all to the good of Singapore seeking to invent itself and remain competitive in the global market." He constantly challenges his students to reach their intellectual limits and encourages them to think out of the box so much so that they affectionately dub him 'The Intellectual Terrorist'.

His knowledge of East Asian economies came in handy when he was appointed the Ambassador to South Korea. There, he was very impressed by the respect which the country conferred on academics.

He was equally at home in Brussels, the headquarters of the European Union. In London, he wore a bowler hat and tuxedo when he was driven by horse and carriage to present his credentials to the Queen. He recalls how a Singapore student once asked him when his office of High Commission would be upgraded to an Embassy.

He gives some interesting insights into his two different careers. "In diplomacy, one was working in an organisation to advance the interests of a country. In academia, institutional interests mattered less and the academic could happily pursue his own individual professional goals. With its focus on independent research and data gathering, academia undervalued negotiating, interpersonal and team-building skills, which I quickly learned were indispensable to the craft of diplomacy. The former puts a premium on intensive research and reflection, whereas in the latter, the time horizon was more compressed."

Pang Eng Fong is neither the absent-minded professor nor the suave diplomat who zealously observes protocol. He yearns for new challenges and likes to explore and discover. His love for adventure has taken him to far-flung parts of Central Asia, where he volunteers his expertise to the Sasakawa Foundation to set up tertiary institutions in the newly independent countries.

He is someone who does not take the conventional route. On holiday trips, he would sometimes drive his friends crazy by always venturing off the beaten track. "I like to take the less travelled road," he jokes. Neither is he cramped by the trappings of his office. At official functions, he would be dressed in an expensive suit, but not without his trademark haversack, which contains his acrostic puzzle, camera and mobile phone which he never switches on. His favourite haunt is Beauty World, where he eats and shops, as he does not believe in patronising posh restaurants and shopping centres. His reading is eclectic and he goes to bed with a book. He is a converted evolutionist in the Charles Darwin mould and he also has a passion for electronic gadgetry.

Pang Eng Fong delights in the unusual and the unexpected. At times, he may appear to be enigmatic and iconoclastic, but nothing could be further from the truth for he is a serious, thinking individual, acutely aware of his responsibilities and actions. He is a human being with a sense of humour, doing the best he can, with abundant humility and modesty.

Guardian of the Civil Service

Phay Seng Whatt

Phay Seng Whatt gave up his medical practice to serve the Public Service Commission. He had the formidable task of reforming, restructuring and streamlining the public service in the newly self-governing Singapore.

Phay was born in Johore. When his family moved to Singapore, he attended Tuan Mong School. Later, his father moved him to Victoria School. He had no idea about his future. His friend, Eu Chooi Yip advised him to study Medicine. Latin was a compulsory subject which was not taught at the Victoria School. So, he sat for an examination and was admitted into RI. His classmates already had two years' grounding in Latin. Nevertheless, he persevered and obtained a distinction in the Junior Cambridge Examinations. He was awarded a scholarship worth $60. With this princely sum, he supplemented the family budget.

Phay's studies at the King Edward VII College were interrupted by the Japanese Occupation. His father had also died. So, he had to support his siblings, planting vegetables and rearing poultry. These hardships strengthened his resolve to succeed in life. He resumed his studies after the War and graduated with distinction.

He worked in Middleton Hospital and General Hospital, before starting his own practice in 1952 where he practised for the next ten years.

His life took an unexpected turn in 1962 when he was appointed Chairman of the Public Service Commission. He had already served as a member for two years. So he gave up his lucrative practice for the much lower monthly salary of $2,300. "Singapore had just achieved self-government. It was our privilege to serve our country. As the Chairman, I shunned publicity and was hardly in the news." He also declined the offer of an official car and a driver.

His immediate task was to cleanse the public image of the Civil Service. A new Corrupt Practices Investigation Bureau was established. "The Commission had to grapple with the multifaceted problems of administration, training, scholarships and promotions." It was given the unenviable task of shaking up the Civil Service and streamlining it into an efficient institution. "I introduced the Merit Promotion Scheme, whereby bright young men and women could be adequately rewarded, so that they would remain in the Service."

He was also responsible for planning and projecting Singapore's manpower needs. He ensured that the best students were awarded with the most prestigious scholarships.

Phay Seng Whatt is reputed for transforming the Civil Service into an incorruptible and responsible institution. For his signal contribution, he was awarded the Distinguished Service Order. He was also conferred the honorary degree of DLitt by the University of Singapore.

The Lady is a Judge

Judith Prakash

Judith Evelyn Jyothi Prakash belongs to the new generation of woman lawyers who have risen to the top of their profession. Now, a High Court Judge, she still recalls her schooldays when she used to dance the rock 'n' roll.

She took a circuitous route via schools such as Siglap Primary, Opera Estate Girls, Dunearn Integrated Secondary and Marymount Convent, before she was admitted into Raffles Girls' School in 1968. "It was my ambition to go to RGS ever since I was in primary school. RGS was known then, as it is known now, as the best girls' school in Singapore. I was drawn to the school by its reputation for academic excellence." Yet, Judith Prakash would not have passed through the portals of RGS, if not for a strange twist of Fate. It coincided with the time when RGS was offering pre-university classes. Traditionally, most of the girls would have proceeded to RI. Also, her father, Gerald De Cruz, was in the RI Queen's Scholarship Class of 1936.

"Once in RGS, I found that it had so much to offer me than just its academic programme. I found dedicated and caring teachers and a committed Principal in Miss Norris. I always got on well with her. Also, a marvellous school spirit, and cohorts who were stimulating and intelligent. My classmates and I were soon caught up in the whole range of interesting and challenging activities."

Judith was prominent in drama and debate. She wrote plays and acted in the *Raffles Players*' production of Shakespeare's *A Winter's Tale*. Being a formidable debater, she was a member of the RGS team which took part in the first-ever series of inter-school debates. She was also a member of the victorious team which won the television series of inter-school quizzes.

As a teenage schoolgirl, Judith had her fair share of fun and pranks. One of her most endearing memories was being taught to dance the rock 'n' roll by a gyrating classmate. They had seized the opportunity when the teacher was at a staff meeting. On another occasion, they held a beauty parade in the class — to determine who had the best pair of legs.

Judith entered the University of Singapore in 1970. An outstanding student, she crowned her brilliant academic record with a First Class Honours in Law. She was in private practice until 1992, when she was appointed a Judicial Commissioner. She became a High Court Judge in 1995. Her husband, Jaya, is a lawyer and a Rotarian. He was a prefect, the President of the Interact Club and he was also on the editorial board of *The Rafflesian*. The couple had their first encounter at the first ever inter-school televised debate in 1969. Their romance blossomed when they both read Law at the University of Singapore. "I asked Jaya whether it was love at first sight." He said, "Well, it took a little bit of time."

She still maintains her close links with her *alma mater*, teachers and classmates, heading its Board of Governors. RGS can be justifiably proud that it is being guided by the dynamic and inspiring leadership of one of its most distinguished graduates.

An Honourable Man

A. P. Rajah

Arumugam Ponnurajah was a lawyer, politician, diplomat and judge. He was affectionately known to his friends and colleagues as A. P. Rajah. He brought to the various high offices that he held his own inimitable warmth, sensitivity, charm, urbane wit and sense of humanity.

Rajah was born in Port Dickson, Negri Sembilan, in 1911. His father came to Malaya in 1905 and was the President of the Asian Planters Association. He was educated at St John's Institution in Kuala Lumpur and St Paul's Institution in Seremban. He completed his pre-university education at Raffles Institution. He represented Raffles at hockey, soccer and cricket, where he was an awesome fast bowler. He proceeded to Raffles College and read Law at Lincoln's College, Oxford University. He graduated in 1932 and was called to the English Bar. In 1938, he was admitted to the Straits Settlements Bar and established his own law practice. He was a Municipal Commissioner and City Councillor. He was also a member of the University of Malaya Council and Trustee of the Singapore Improvement Trust.

Rajah was a founder member of the Progressive Party, which later merged with the Democratic Party to form the Liberal-Socialist Party. After the 1955 General Election, he parted company with them. He successfully contested the 1959 General Election to the Legislative Assembly as an Independent, and later allied himself with the Singapore People's Alliance Party. A sound politician, highly respected by all for his integrity and honesty of purpose, he was a fearless critic of the PAP government. Nevertheless, he was a staunch supporter of the merger of Singapore with Malaya. In 1963, after losing his Farrer Park seat, he retired from politics.

His appointment in 1964 as Speaker of the Legislative Assembly was the highest accolade accorded by the PAP to a former formidable opponent in the Assembly. On the merger issue, he had stood by what he believed was right, regardless of Party interests. When Singapore attained Independence in 1965, he became the first Speaker of Parliament.

After completing two years as Speaker, Rajah began an eight-year term as a diplomat. It was with a sense of *déjà vu* when he returned to London, as Singapore's High Commissioner to the United Kingdom. He was also High Commissioner to Australia and Fiji. As a diplomat, he represented his country, then a new and fledgling nation, in a manner which brought credit and respect not only to himself, but also to Singapore.

In 1976, Rajah was appointed a Supreme Court Judge. As a judge, he constantly urged lawyers to be mindful of human frailty and the human aspect of legal problems. He graciously imparted to the legal profession his vast knowledge and experience, derived from his work as an advocate and solicitor.

He has made significant contributions to the community through his service in various capacities since 1947. He was the Chairman of the Hindu Advisory Board and advocated the resumption of the teaching of the Tamil language in the university. He was also interested in Chinese art and porcelain. For his distinguished public service, he was appointed a Pro-Chancellor of the National University of Singapore and conferred the honorary degree of Doctor of Law by the university.

Rajah is greatly respected for his integrity and humanity. He always played the game of a true sportsman, one who was never afraid to say "It isn't cricket" against what he considered to be unfair and unjust.

Deadly Striker

Quah Kim Song

Quah Kim Song represented Singapore in football when he was only a schoolboy at the age of 17. His greatest triumph came in 1977 when he scored the winning goal against Penang, which enabled Singapore to win the Malaysia Cup after a 13-year drought. His deadly strike made him a national icon to thousands of his adoring fans, who had almost given up any hope of Singapore ever winning the Malaysia Cup again.

Quah received his education from Canberra Primary School, Naval Base Secondary School and Raffles Institution (1969–1970). In those two years, Raffles reigned supreme on the football field and was invincible against all the other schools. He recalls one particular match against St Joseph's Institution at the Jalan Besar Stadium. "We won 4-0. I scored two goals. After the match, we were surrounded by the opposition fans who harassed me and wanted to pick a fight. I laughed it off and told them that it was only a game and that they should accept the result gracefully and not resort to such unruly behaviour." A potentially ugly incident was averted. He was initiated into football by his older brothers, five of whom have had represented Singapore. From them, the young Kim Song learned how to be magnanimous in victory and sporting in defeat. Throughout his football career, he always heeded their advice.

For more than a decade, he strode the football scene like a Colossus, outmanouevring and mesmerising his opponents and leaving them for dead as he surged and sped towards their goal, shooting the ball into the net. He generated electricity whenever the ball was at his feet. He was the supreme artist who performed magic with a mere turn of his supple body or a deft flick, and held the thousands of spectators spellbound. With him spearheading the Singapore attack, Quah's fame was frequently highlighted in the sports pages of newspapers. He spawned a new generation of loyal supporters who fervently followed Singapore's chances of regaining the Malaysia Cup, which was proving very elusive. They had to wait several years. It was only in 1977 that their hopes were realised. Singapore defeated Penang 3-2 at the Merdeka Stadium. Quah scored two goals, including the crucial winner in extra time. Singapore had emerged as champion after a lapse of 13 years. For Quah, it was a personal triumph as he was on the losing side the year before. It was also a vindication of his indomitable spirit and his tribute to his many fans. "During the Malaysia Cup campaigns, I always looked forward to the matches to showcase my skills and to delight the thousands who had come to support us, rain or shine."

Off the football field, he held executive positions in the corporate world. He uses his expertise in his present post as Chief of Competitions with the Football Association of Singapore. His responsibilities include looking after all the domestic and international tournaments.

How does he view the present state of Singapore football? "The task ahead is monumental. It's not easy to handle players and parents of today. It's difficult to convince youngsters to think of football as a career fraught with many problems. What we are doing now will benefit Singapore football many years down the road. We are putting in the infrastructure and gradually, but surely, making inroads into getting more and more youngsters to come forward."

Quah Kim Song is cautiously optimistic for the future of Singapore football. As a member of the famous Quah family, no one can doubt his commitment and passion for this national game. Like another Rafflesian, Chia Boon Leong, before him, Quah Kim Song is a legend in the annals of Singapore football.

Author of National Pledge

S. Rajaratnam

Sinnathamby Rajaratnam is one of the founding fathers of an independent Singapore. His life was devoted to building Singapore into a multiracial nation, uniting people of diverse ethnicities and cultures.

He was born in Ceylon (Sri Lanka) in 1915 and received his early education at St Paul's Institution in Seremban, Victoria Institution in Kuala Lumpur, and Raffles Institution. He then continued his studies at King's College in London. His university studies were, however, interrupted by the War. He was Associate Editor of the *Singapore Standard* from 1950 to 1954 and was also on the editorial staff of *The Straits Times.* He was a founder member and President of the National Union of Journalists. In 1955, he sat on the Malayanisation Commission.

Rajaratnam was a convenor and founder member of the People's Action Party. In 1959, he was elected to the Legislative Assembly for the Kampong Glam Constituency and was appointed Minister for Culture. A member of the Central Executive Committee and Director of the Political Bureau, he was returned in 1963. With the formation of Malaysia in 1963, he became a member of the Malaysian Federal Parliament. In 1965, when Singapore separated from Malaysia, he became Minister for Foreign Affairs. He was also Minister for Labour from 1968 to 1971, and Second Deputy Prime Minister, Foreign Affairs, retiring from active politics in 1988. After his retirement from politics, he joined the Institute of Southeast Asian Studies as a Senior Fellow.

Rajaratnam was a pioneering author of Malayan short stories in the 1950s. As Minister for Culture, he launched the *Aneka Rengam Raayat* or cultural road shows. He played a leading role in the advent of television, which was crucial in winning the hearts and minds of the masses in the battle for merger with Malaysia. Rajaratnam's book, *PAP — First Ten Years,* has become a classic document for researchers of contemporary Singapore political history.

An avid reader, he was regularly seen browsing in bookshops. A prolific writer, he was fond of coining new slogans and was the first to call Singapore a 'global city'.

On 9 August 1965, when Singapore separated from Malaysia, Rajaratnam was the obvious choice for the Foreign Affairs portfolio. As Foreign Minister, he established his reputation internationally as the eloquent, perceptive statesman. At the United Nations General Assembly, the Non-Aligned Conference or at the ASEAN Foreign Ministers Meeting, his speeches displayed a quality of unyielding strength and logic. His vast knowledge, charm and friendliness helped him to win many friends for Singapore.

Rajaratnam was in the forefront for a 'Malaysian Malaysia' but he was abruptly disillusioned in 1965. He said, "I believe in multiracialism. Separation to me was the crushing of my dreams. I believe in one nation, regardless of race and religion. My dreams were shattered."

To Rajaratnam, Lee Kuan Yew was the pre-eminent leader. He confirmed that Lee was a dominant man. "He does not act on consensus. Once he has decided, that's it." But he asserted that although it had been the rule of a strong man, it is a pragmatism which had made Singapore work. "My contributions were very abstract. There are no buildings that I can point to and say they are what I did. I was supposed to be there, helping to shape people's ideas, attitudes, thinking up propaganda, cultural presentations."

Sinnathamby Rajaratnam has been described as one of Lee Kuan Yew's most trusted lieutenants. He was Singapore's longest serving Foreign Minister. His enduring legacy is the National Pledge which he drafted. His kindness and unassuming air made him much loved. He was accorded a state funeral when he died on 22 February 2006, three days short of his 91st birthday.

Mr Mayor

Zainul Abidin Rasheed

Zainul Abidin Rasheed is a Mayor with the common touch. His North East Community Development Council handles the collective responsibility of looking after 700,000 people. A highly respected leader in the Malay community, he passionately believes in a multiracial Singapore. In his varied career as a trade unionist, journalist, community leader and politician, he is constantly reminded of the experiences and lessons he had learned as a schoolboy. They became invaluable preparation for his adult life.

Zainul was born in 1948. "My house was situated somewhere between Joo Chiat and Geylang, an area full of heritage, history and nostalgia. Joo Chiat was always known as a black area in the early days of race relations. During the racial riots, we were really caught in a very difficult position."

He studied in a Malay school and also in Jalan Daud and Opera Estate Primary before joining RI where he studied from 1962 to 1967. He was a Green Cord Scout, a librarian, and was active in sports as well as the Interact Club. He graduated in Political Science from the University of Singapore, where he was also editor of the student paper *The Undergrad*.

Zainul said that RI helped him to see himself as a Singaporean. "It had a very multiracial setting and which was interwoven with its activities, my friends and teachers. I was on the pioneering Board of Governors, when RI was going independent. My friends told me that I must ensure that RI does not become elitist or cater for only certain racial or economic groups. We should retain what RI was in terms of the mix of students. That is the strength of RI. In fact, as I speak this, I get goose pimples. Those are the values we want to inculcate. I'm very lucky that my three sons and one daughter are Rafflesians. We savour and endorse the Rafflesian spirit, which I hope will remain forever."

Zainul Abidin was profoundly shocked by the 1964 riots when he was in Secondary 3. "I was almost killed that day. I saw Malays and Indians being maimed with iron bars and acid bulbs. I managed to escape and returned to Geylang. There, I saw Malays attacking Chinese trishaw riders and hawkers. It was there and then that I told myself that I would do my utmost to ensure that the carnage will never be repeated."

The seeds of his concern for his fellow Singaporeans were already planted when Zainul was only a primary schoolboy at Jalan Daud. "I was in charge of the UNICEF free milk programme. Every morning, I would stir the milk and give it to the poor. The children who lined up for milk had all come without breakfast. Even till now, I can still see on their faces what it's like to be poor. It made me realise that there will always be people who need help. We must not forget them, whether in the context of Singapore or other countries. We are able to help these people, as we have done for the tsunami and earthquake victims."

In the trade union movement, Zainul managed the NTUC FairPrice enterprise and administered the Singapore Port Workers Union. He began his journalism career by editing the *Asia Research Bulletin*, then *Berita Harian* and *The Straits Times*. A natural Malay leader, he takes a lead role in MUIS and Mendaki. In the area of politics, he is a Member of Parliament for the Aljunied GRC. He was Senior Parliamentary Secretary before becoming Minister of State for Foreign Affairs and the Mayor of the North East Community Development Council. "As Mayor, I can really be in touch with the ground. I can reach out to the people and understand their feelings, aspirations and frustrations. I try to bridge their aspirations and reality through bonding programmes, education and financial assistance, quality of life, and even entrepreneurship and creativity."

Zainul Abidin Rasheed is a staunch champion and practitioner for a multiracial Singapore. "We have certain sensitivities and interests to look after. We are in the process of forging a cohesive society. Along the way, there will be rough edges and we have to manage them."

Zainul Abidin Rasheed is undoubtedly a down-to-earth Mayor who grapples with the daily problems of the community. "This is my heart line, my lifeline — wanting to work and serve others. I think this is reflected in all that I have been doing. The seeds of my social conscience and awareness were sown when I was a very young boy distributing free milk and also when I was in RI."

International Art Historian

T. Kanaga Sabapathy

T. Kanaga Sabapathy is one of the most respected and highly regarded art historians in Southeast Asia. As a historian, curator, critic and adviser he has influenced artistic opinion and shaped knowledge of visual art for over 30 years. He is in his element when he extols the beauty and splendour of Angkor Wat and Borobodur to rapt audiences. His love for antiquity belies his prowess as a rugged sportsman when he was a young man. Kanaga was a national schoolboy champion miler. He also represented Singapore in hockey.

Kanaga learned his hockey, playing with 25 other *kampong* boys. The field was the size of a badminton court. He mastered the skills of dribbling and stick work. From Serangoon English School, he proceeded to Raffles, where he achieved athletic fame. He emulated the feats of the school's legend, J. K. Mitra, in the long distance races. "I trained for three months, running for an hour every day."

He readily admits that Raffles enabled him to develop to his full potential, as a young man and later, as an adult. "I remember that Monday morning in January 1955 very vividly. It was a day when I was stepping out into the world, a day of anticipation and some trepidation. I alighted from the 40-minute bus ride. I had arrived at the Centre. In my reckoning, it marked a mighty leap from the *kampong* to the city. It marked a vaulting leap away from innocence, towards being savvy. The RI experience was varied, fulfilling and formative as entire worlds were unrolled. Our teachers appeared larger than life. Their erudition and personalities were encompassing. They demonstrated the power of language in shaping the world, in embodying knowledge and in articulating thought processes. They left an enduring impression on me, affecting my approach to scholarship and teaching."

On the sports field, Kanaga was in the select company of brilliant all-rounders, including Ridgeway Ponnampalam, Balderaj Singh and Gan Boon Leong, who was the national 120-yards hurdles champion. A prefect and actor with the *Raffles Players*, Kanaga teamed up with Ellen and Harry Crabbe.

"Delicate connections were woven between friends, fuelling our interests in learning and enriching grounds for living. We were unafraid to assert a sense of ourselves, uninhibited in giving expression to our world views. We were conscious of being on the crest of momentous times in history. Raffles Institution fostered and shaped our ideals and lives." Kanaga graduated in History from the University of Malaya in Singapore in 1961. He was the University's hockey captain.

He is currently an Adjunct Professor in the Department of Architecture at the National University of Singapore after having been a lecturer in the History of Art for the past 25 years. He is much sought after for his advisory work by museums and other public and educational institutions, nationally and regionally. His early professional engagements were marked by clear commitments to the Art Historiography of the grand traditions of Southeast Asian art. He later emerged as an eloquent proponent for assessing modern and contemporary Southeast Asian art within specific contexts, assessing the dignity and centrality of their histories and development. His art historical method, critical interpretation and detailed explications of the works of key artists have defined Singaporean and Malaysian art. His numerous publications and extensive studies have added visual intelligibility and intellectual depth to art discourses in the region. He is also the founding Director of Asia Contemporary, an independent facility for advancing research of modern and contemporary art in Southeast Asia.

T. Kanaga Sabapathy has devoted his lifetime's work to the history of art in Southeast Asia. Through his scholarship, research and teaching, he is a giant in a very specialised profession. However, he is modest about his achievements. "I consider myself a freak, as I don't think that anyone else has given as much time and effort to the subject."

He is a romantic, always striving for truth and beauty, with his critical artistic eye. He nostalgically recalls his childhood, bridging the past with the present, tinged with bitter-sweet memories. "Today, we live in conditions that are designed, regulated and urbanised completely. In these circumstances, it is difficult to picture a Singapore that is made up of a country-city divide. It was real then. Travelling from home, which was in the heart of Tampines, then an extensive coconut plantation, to school, was to journey through different geographies. The topography altered, as did the vegetation and the light, while passing along the seemingly unending Serangoon Road. On passing Rochor Canal and entering Selegie Road, the country slipped away into the precincts that formed the city. Raffles Institution virtually marked the centre of the city."

There is still very much the schoolboy in T. Kanaga Sabapathy.

Television Personality

V. Sadasivan

Viswa Sadasivan was a very familiar face on Singapore television for many years. He anchored and presented programmes, such as *Talking Point, Feedback* and *Today in Parliament,* and also covered and directed parliamentary reports and the General Elections. In his 24 years of television experience, he held top posts in the Singapore Broadcasting Corporation, Singapore Press Holdings and UTV International. He was Chairman of the Right Angle group of companies until March 2007. Since then, he formed Strategic Moves — a strategic crisis and communications training, and corporate strategy consultancy firm for top management in Fortune 500 companies as well as in Singapore's public sector. If this was not enough, in May 2007, Viswa started up yet another company with a partner. Called MagikAsia, it strives to create and distribute showcase animation features, and create innovative content in the new media and Interactive Digital Media (IDM) space that will help put Singapore on the world map.

Viswa attended Cantonment Primary School and was at Raffles Institution during the years 1972 to 1977, where he represented the school in tennis and hockey. As a Boy Scout, he was reputed for his ability to mimic the mating sound of a chicken. He participated in oratorical contests and acted in prominent roles in the *Raffles Players.* He recalls his debut in Shakespeare's *Macbeth* where during the banquet scene, he had to balance three apples on a paper plate, which to his horror, tumbled down to the floor. "There must be easier and more dignified ways to fame," he jokes. His initial stage fright did not deter him from becoming a famous television personality in his adult life. "I am grateful to my teachers for nurturing my talent for the arts. Mr Philip Liau was the epitome of the Rafflesian spirit. He told us that we should not be arrogant about being in RI. Rather, we should be humble to have been given the privilege. Also, I owe a lot to my parents for instilling in me a strong sense of community spirit and an appreciation of current affairs from a tender age."

Viswa graduated in Political Science from the University of Singapore in 1983 and obtained his Master in Public Administration from Harvard in 1992. He started his career with the Singapore Broadcasting Corporation in 1983, where he found his niche in television, for which he had a natural talent. He held the posts of Producer, Editor and finally that of Senior Controller, Current Affairs Division in 1995. "*Feedback* and *Talking Point* became highly popular programmes. They earned the people's trust and people started speaking up on issues and concerns. Even today, total strangers will discuss current issues with me because they remember me and trust me. This is one of the greatest rewards that a TV presenter can hope to get. I have always been a firm believer in working within the system to open up space for discussion and discourse. I believe that we can debate and state our point of view without being combative and disrupting political stability. For a society to grow and mature and attain a psychological resilience necessary for the challenges ahead, we need to get people to become active in thought and action. For this to happen, they must feel that they are respected partners in building our nation." This was the impetus for Viswa to serve as Chairman, Political Development, Feedback Unit for eight years. In addition, he served on key national committees such as the Economic Review Committee, Remaking Singapore Committee and Singapore 21 Committee, and as a Resource Panel member of the Government Parliamentary Committee on Defence and Foreign Affairs.

As the Senior Manager of Corporate Planning of the Singapore Press Holdings, he was instrumental in laying the groundwork for its venture into the television industry.

Given his achievements in SBC, and subsequently with SPH and then UTV International, and then as an entrepreneur who pioneered one of the most established independent production companies in

Singapore — Viswa Sadasivan is held in high regard as a doyen of the media industry. For this reason he was appointed to the Board of the Media Development Authority for four years.

Given his standing, deep knowledge and analytical powers, there is no surprise that Viswa is a respected political commentator in the local media.

As a consultant, he is sought after for his knack for developing simple but effective strategies for corporations to achieve their goals. Viswa was engaged by Las Vegas Sands Corp to serve as strategic advisor for their S$5 billion bid for the Marina Bay IR — which they clinched.

Viswa Sadasivan's expertise and experience is sought after for community work and engagement. In this regard, he has served on many boards, including as Secretary of SINDA's Executive Committee where he has been serving for more than 11 years. Viswa makes it a point to spend time with young people with ideas and passion — to mentor and counsel them. "I view my community service as a form of paying back to society for giving me many opportunities in life and for the privilege of studying in Singapore's premier school. Fame and fortune is one thing. But the feeling you get when you know you have touched a life, and made a difference — ah, that feeling is the ultimate reward."

Viswa Sadasivan is surely a media entrepreneur with a social conscience!

Pioneering Stage Actress

Rosie Seow

Rosie Seow was a pioneering stage actress in the 1950s, when Singapore's English language theatre was in its infancy. The drama world was then dominated by the British expatriate community. In the 1950s and 60s, she acted under her stage name of 'Kheng Lim'.

Rosie was born in 1922 and educated at Raffles Girls' School and Raffles College, when her studies were interrupted by the Second World War. She was the daughter of Seow Poh Leng, a prominent banker. She was introduced to drama at a very early age by her parents. In 1940, Raffles College produced Oscar Wilde's *The Importance Of Being Earnest.* She played the role of Miss Prism, opposite Lee Kuan Yew, who acted as Canon Chasuble.

In 1952, Rosie attended London's famous drama school, the Royal Academy of Dramatic Arts. She was highly praised for being one of its best students. On returning to Singapore, she acted in many plays, mainly Shakespearean. Her most memorable role was as the spritely Ariel in *The Tempest.* She also acted as 'Silver Stream' in *Lady Precious Stream,* the first English language play which was based on a Chinese opera.

As a teacher in the Singapore Chinese Girls' School for several years, she inculcated in her students, the love for English literature and drama. She took pains to ensure that they read, write and speak good English and was very particular with their pronunciation and diction.

For Rosie Seow and the other pioneers of English theatre in the 1950s, acting was essentially a labour of love. The small group of enthusiasts were drawn mainly from university academics and British expatriates from Radio Malaya and the armed forces. The actors sewed their own costumes and painted the sets themselves. Tickets were priced at $2 and the plays seldom drew a full house. Rare advertisements for programmes were solicited through friends and well-wishers. There was no government funding and corporate sponsorship was unheard of then. The plays that were staged were usually Shakespearean and English classics.

The stage was the poor relative of the cinema, which attracted bigger audiences to its silver screen. The actors and their patrons formed the minority of a minority. It was an era when the Chinese masses flocked to the street *wayang*. Malay and Indian communities also had their fair share of drama and cultural activities.

Today, English theatre in Singapore owes a debt of gratitude to pioneers like Rosie Seow. They courageously persevered and kept theatre alive in the 1950s against great odds. Their pioneering efforts have not been in vain, for their sacrifices have spawned the present generation of promising playwrights, actors, dramatists, choreographers and poets.

For Rosie Seow, it was a source of personal pride that she had nurtured and inspired her daughter, Stella Kon, to become one of Singapore's leading playwrights.

Father of Obstetrics and Gynaecology

Benjamin Henry Sheares

Benjamin Henry Sheares is affectionately regarded as the father of Obstetrics and Gynaecology in Singapore. He was undoubtedly one of the most illustrious graduates of the King Edward VII College of Medicine, who pioneered a procedure which is named after him. He was made Singapore's second President, in recognition of his distinguished service.

He was born on 12 August 1907, the son of a Public Works Department technical supervisor. He was educated at Methodist Girls' School, St Andrew's School and Raffles Institution and graduated as a doctor at the very young age of 22. His initial intention was to specialise in Internal Medicine, but instead, he was posted to an outpatient clinic in Malacca for two years. He requested for a transfer and was told that the only vacancy available was at the Kandang Kerbau Maternity Hospital. Later, he admitted that he did not choose Obstetrics and Gynaecology, but once he was involved in this area of specialisation, he loved it tremendously.

Although he was awarded the Queen's Scholarship, he could not pursue it until 1947 because of the War. He topped his class and was the first Singaporean to be admitted to the membership of the Royal College. In 1950, he became the first Professor of Obstetrics and Gynaecology and during his tenure, he made childbirth safe for both mother and child.

Sheares was conferred the degrees of Doctor of Medicine and Master of Surgery by the University of Malaya in Singapore. After leaving the university, he became the Honorary Consultant at the

Kandang Kerbau Hospital. He was a dedicated teacher and was much loved by his junior staff and students. The *Kandang Kerbau Hospital Bulletin*, the forerunner of the *Journal of Obstetrics and Gynaecology*, was started by him. He also headed the Family Planning Association and the Family Planning and Population Board. In the 1960s when Singapore's birth rate was spiralling beyond control, he advocated voluntary sterilisation.

Sheares was conferred numerous honours and awards for his medical expertise, including those from Indonesia and Malaysia. His highest honour came when he served as Singapore's second President from 1971 to 1981. The Benjamin Sheares Bridge, one of Singapore's famous landmarks, is a lasting memorial of his distinguished service to the nation.

As the Head of State, he was conscientious and very devoted to his numerous duties. He led by example and his keen intellect and quiet dignity inspired both Singaporeans and visiting dignitaries. In his weekly lectures at the Kandang Kerbau Hospital, he dispensed with protocol, much to the chagrin of the hospital authorities, who were at the same time, bemused by his informality and humility.

Sheares' humble and unassuming ways belied an intense commitment to excellence. A master clinician, he took great pains over his lectures to his students and staff, who were privileged to be taught by him. He had a good pair of hands and they took every opportunity to learn his child delivery and operating techniques. Few could equal his surgical skills and he pioneered the Sheares operation for the reconstruction of the vagina. Kandang Kerbau Hospital was his pride and joy, indeed his second home. He displayed his dedication and perfectionist outlook to the end of his working days. Whereas men younger than him would have retired, he continued to lecture, despite his state duties and failing health.

Sheares died on 12 May 1981 at the age of 73 and thousands of people from all walks of life went to the Istana to pay their last respects to their President and to a great man. The Kandang Kerbau Hospital staff not only paid their last respects at the Istana, but also lined part of the route at Bukit Timah Road for a last look at their leader as the gun carriage passed by, before his body was laid to rest at the State Cemetery at Kranji.

The Monk Who Came in from the Cold

Shi Ming Yi

Ming Yi was born in 1962 and was twenty-eight when he became the abbot of the Foo Hai Ch'an Monastery in Geylang East in 1990. He was previously attached to a small temple in Mountbatten Road. The old temple was a small two-storey building and in need of much repair. It was then that he had his bold vision. Instead of repairing it, he dreamt of building a new one and making it an open sanctuary for meditation and contemplation. He envisaged a Tang-style temple complex, like those in Japan. He realised that there was a growing number of people, especially the young, who were interested in Buddhism.

Ming Yi clearly saw the urgency of his calling, not only to sit and meditate and seek his own enlightenment. He decided to play a more active and public role as the people's guide to the ancient contemplative traditions and the model of compassion with its teachers.

Venerable Shi Ming Yi felt that for too long, Buddhism had been associated with ancestor worship, smoky temples, unrecognisable gods and incomprehensible rituals. A new post-Independence generation had grown up, which did not associate Buddhism and ancestor worship with poverty and backwardness. The 1980s also heralded a new era of globalisation and technology, which brought about uncertainty and disorientating changes. More people were turning to religion in order to cope and to find solace. "Buddhism is not just about theory, but also practice. You have to use your hands to help people."

The $16 million Tang-style Foo Hai Ch'an Monastery was completed after four years in 2000, complete with multipurpose facilities which included a prayer hall, lodgings, auditorium, meditation rooms and recording studios. Ming Yi's dream had been fulfilled, thanks to the generosity of the many benefactors and well-wishers. But much of the credit should go to Ming Yi himself. He was the inspiration for its design, planning and fund-raising.

A ten-metre high bronze statue of Kuan Yin stands in the temple grounds. It was designed and moulded in China and cast in Japan. Ming Yi explained why Kuan Yin is within a Zen temple. "Most Singaporeans are used to the image of Kuan Yin. The 1,000 hands suggest compassion. We help as many people as we can." Kuan Yin is the Chinese version of Avalokitesvara (in Sanskrit).

He also founded the Ren Ci Hospital for the chronic sick in 1994. Recently, he has built a second hospital. He became well known for his spectacular fund-raising efforts, even beyond Buddhist circles. He is also the Secretary-General of the Singapore Buddhist Federation and adviser to religious institutions and schools. He is much sought after as a speaker because of his charisma and because he is effectively bilingual.

In 1996, the Singapore government awarded the Public Service Medal to Venerable Shi in recognition of his contributions to the country.

World-Renowned Violinist

Siow Lee Chin

Siow Lee Chin is a world-renowned violinist. A child prodigy and now only in her thirties, she has performed with many famous conductors and orchestras in many leading cities of the world. She is the Professor of Strings in the University of Charleston, North Carolina, in the United States.

Siow studied in Raffles Girls' School from 1979 to 1982. Her father is a former member of the Singapore Symphony Orchestra. He gave Lee Chin a violin when she was only three months old. "I became interested when I saw my father's students playing the violin and it seemed such fun making music in a group. But I did not like practising." Under her father's tutelage, she obtained her Associated Board of the Royal School of Music Grade 8 qualification, just three years after her first violin lesson. A precocious 12-year-old, she filled in for the SSO when it fell short of violinists. "My feet could barely touch the ground while I was trying to keep time." Her talent was spotted by the visiting professor of The Curtis Institute of Music, who offered her a place in the Institute. It was the opportunity of a lifetime and the 16-year-old Lee Chin did not hesitate. Her father was supportive, although her mother was naturally concerned. The rest is history.

Her studies at Curtis were amply sponsored by the Loke Foundation. In Philadelphia, she quickly learned to fend for herself and be independent. She graduated with a Bachelor of Music in 1988 and won a scholarship to the Mannes College of Music in New York City, where she obtained her Masters in 1992. She made her debut at the Carnegie Hall in 1991, as part of her prize for winning the Artistes International Competition. The coveted engagement was a nerve-racking experience for her as she was a foreigner and had to compete with other equally talented and eager musicians. The prestigious venue is a springboard for aspiring artistes.

For more than a decade, the glamorous young violinist has travelled the globe and charmed and enthralled audiences everywhere. Strikingly fair with fine features and long hair that cascades down slim shoulders, Lee Chin cuts a pretty picture in the competitive world of performing arts, where good looks could be an added advantage. But once on stage, it is her talent that would be on show. A critic wrote that Siow has both fire and ice in her temperament. "I must say I'm very passionate about my music. I like Russian music, with its strong temperament. As for icy, I suppose he means coolness." She has been hailed as a violinist who possesses superb control with tasteful flair. She is also described as a rising star with powerful artistic temperament and electrifying technique.

Siow Lee Chin has a distinguished career as a soloist. She is currently the Professor of Strings in the Music Department of the University of Charleston. She feels that she has partially made the transition between primarily working as a performer and focusing on her role as a teacher. "When you teach, you are always putting the students first. But, when you perform, you are always thinking of yourself, how you feel, how will your audience accept you. It's always me, me, me. Very narcissistic and self-centred."

At the relatively young age of 37, Siow Lee Chin has already reached the pinnacle of her profession, She can afford to bask in her glory and accomplishments as she is on top of the world. But she is philosophical on how music has transformed her life. "Everything I have learned in life has been because of music. Growing up, for any difficulties I had, I turned to music to help solve them. Music teaches you patience because things don't always work out the way you want and you have to keep trying over and over. I know everything happens for a reason. I recognise the challenge when I reach the plateau and I relish it."

Beautiful and talented Siow Lee Chin has conquered the hearts of many concert audiences around the world. She has now made a transition from performing to teaching. We wish her great success in her new musical career and hope that one day, she will return to teach at our Yong Siew Toh Conservatory of Music.

Father of Amateur Football

Soh Ghee Soon

Soh Ghee Soon was the longest serving President of the Singapore Amateur Football Association in the 1950s. They were the golden years of Singapore football and under his dynamic leadership, Singapore remained the Malaya Cup champion for three years. He was also the founding Vice-President of the Asian Football Confederation. He had a distinguished record in community service and was both a City Councillor as well as an elected member of the Legislative Assembly.

He was born in Singapore in 1903. His daughter, Ivy, tells of a moving story of how the young Ghee Soon got himself admitted to RI. "My father realised the value of belonging to an elite school and receiving a good education. He went to see the Principal himself and convinced him that he would be a good student." At Raffles, Soh Ghee Soon was a champion athlete and boxer. After passing his Junior Cambridge Examinations, he had hoped to pursue further studies but this hope was dashed when his father died. Only fifteen then, he had to support his mother and younger sister. Nevertheless, his education at RI had left an indelible mark on the impressionable schoolboy and those years were useful preparation for his adult life and community service.

As a young boy, Soh quickly learned to fend for himself. His family had moved into the rough neighbourhood of Tanjong Pagar where he was often bullied by the leader of a gang. Undaunted, he took up bodybuilding for a year and challenged the bully to a fight. He got his revenge but his triumph was short-lived as he was promptly caned by his father when he went home.

When the Japanese invaded Singapore in 1942, he was herded into a detention centre with other young men and issued with a paper marked with a cross. Realising that he was in serious danger, he erased the cross with his saliva. He feigned innocence and told the soldier that he had used the paper to wipe his sweaty face. He was slapped and kicked and ordered to kneel in the hot sun but was eventually released.

Soh Ghee Soon was a pioneering advocate for 'a rugged society' and a staunch believer in the saying '*Mens sana in corpore sano*'. In his illustrious lifetime, he played a leading role in as many as 30 sports associations, which included the Bodybuilding Association, the Boxing Association and the Singapore Olympics Sports Council. But his greatest passion was for football. He was the first Singaporean President of the Singapore Amateur Football Association. Under his dynamic leadership, Singapore won the coveted Malaya Cup three times: in 1950, 1952 and 1956. He was affectionately dubbed 'Captain Bligh' because he was a disciplinarian who motivated his players to perform to the best of their ability. As Vice-President of the Asian Football Confederation (AFC), he developed a lasting friendship with Tengku Abdul Rahman, who was the President of the AFC.

He was a City Councillor from 1951 to 1959. In 1955, he was elected to the Legislative Assembly on a Progressive Party ticket for the Cairnhill Constituency. In the 1959 General Election, he lost to the PAP candidate by five votes in River Valley. Always conscious of his humble beginnings, he spoke up for the poor and the underdog.

Despite his stocky, tough guy image, Soh Ghee Soon was a kind and jovial man. He held various executive positions in the private sector, including *The Singapore Standard*. He regularly brought his family to the beach and the movies. He loved to sing and would lead them in his favourite song, *Rosemarie*. His three children, Albert, and two Rafflesian daughters, Ivy and Vivienne, are Arts graduates of what was known then as the University of Malaya.

A Rotarian, he devoted himself to community service and was the Vice-Chairman of the Singapore Anti-Tuberculosis Association. As a sports official, community leader, politician and corporate person, Soh Ghee Soon was highly respected for his honesty, integrity, sportsmanship and sense of fair play. Undoubtedly, these endearing qualities had been inculcated into him when he was a student in Raffles. Soh Ghee Soon is remembered as someone who always fought the good fight and played the game.

The Methodist Bishop

Robert Solomon

Robert Solomon did not pursue his medical profession. Instead, he opted for his vocation as a priest. As the Methodist Bishop, he looks after his flock of 30,000. He also has a doctorate in Pastoral Theology.

Solomon was educated at Labrador Primary and Raffles Institution (1969–1974). He graduated from the University of Singapore with a MBBS in 1980. He received his Theological Studies in Manila and obtained his PhD in Pastoral Theology from Edinburgh University in 1990.

"My education at RI was one of the most significant influences in my life, helping to shape my intellectual, social and psychological development. It gave me a sense of history, studying in a grand institution with a great heritage. Ethnicity was no barrier to the development of close friendships among Raffles boys." He was also the leader of the Red Cross Unit and a school prefect. He also pays tribute to the teachers who moulded his character and interests.

He worked briefly as a medical doctor and left for the Asian Theological Seminary in Manila where he obtained his Masters in Divinity. After receiving his doctorate from Edinburgh University, he joined Trinity Theological College in 1993 and eventually became its Principal. He also served as the pastor of the Tamil Methodist Church in Toa Payoh and in Short Street.

Solomon was elected as the Bishop of the Methodist Church in 2000 at the age of 44. He admits that it was tough for him to quit as a doctor to pursue his theological studies. "At the time, many people told me that it was such a waste. But I had to follow my calling and do what is right to me and to my faith and march to a different drum beat. My medical training and practice have greatly enriched my life. I will help the Church to become not only an active Church, but also a thinking Church to face the new challenges ahead." On his election as Bishop, he sees a three-fold role in his appointment to defend the Faith, preserve unity in the Church, and provide leadership and vision. "I'm glad that I can still teach by preaching from the pulpit or in my writings." He has written four books, which are *Living in Two Worlds, The Hurting Heart, Fire For The Journey* and *Feed My Sheep.*

He does not think that his interests in demon possession are at odds with his medical training. "We tend to think in single dimensions and I have found that it isn't a very useful approach to the complexity of life. I have met people who are psychologically disturbed and are physically unhealthy. So my multidisciplinary training helps me to identify and help them."

Robert Solomon's vocation is a refreshing change in a world which is becoming increasingly preoccupied with materialism and devoid of spirituality. He is an inspiring individual who is not afraid to walk the untrodden path and to follow his calling.

Queen's Scholar

Song Ong Siang

Song Ong Siang (extreme right in photo) was a pioneer in many areas of his endeavours. He was a Queen's Scholar, lawyer, legislator, author and community leader. Born in 1889, Song was one of the most prominent and respected members of the Chinese community. He was the best known Rafflesian of his time.

While studying in RI, he was awarded the Guthrie Scholarship for five consecutive years. This combination of innate brilliance and industry culminated in him obtaining the Queen's Scholarship in 1888. He topped the examinations three times but was disqualified because he did not reach the minimum age of 16 years. He attributed his unbroken academic successes to his School Principal, R. W. Hullett, and his keen rivalry with his close friend, Lim Boon Keng. He graduated from Cambridge with both the LLB and LLM. On returning to Singapore in 1893, he established his own law firm. He was the first Singaporean to be called to the Bar, which was monopolised by expatriates then.

Groomed as a 'King's Chinese', Song was a Lieutenant in the Singapore Volunteer Infantry Regiment and he attended the coronation of King Edward VII. He was a Nominated Member of the Legislative Council in 1936, and he was also decorated a Knight Commander of the Order of Empire, in recognition of his public service.

With Lim Boon Keng, he led the Reform movement within the Chinese community, including the formation of the Philomatic Society. The Straits Chinese magazine was the vehicle for opposing the wearing of the hair queue, opium smoking, foot-binding and concubinage. Song saw education as generating upward social mobility. Realising the plight of the *nonyas* who were confined to the home, he played a leading role in the founding of the Singapore Chinese Girls' School. He also produced *Bintang Timor* in Romanised Malay.

Song died in 1941 at the age of 70, after a lifetime of remarkable achievements. He is best known for his *100 Years' History of the Chinese in Singapore.* He had published his *magnum opus* in celebration of the Colony's centenary. This monumental work bears testimony to his brilliant intellect and historical foresight. He had courageously taken up the challenge, at a time when local writing was non-existent. Originally published in 1902, his pioneering work has stood the test of time and is still an invaluable source for scholars and researchers. It is a fascinating read of the people and personalities who have contributed to the social and economic development of early Singapore. It also gives an interesting insight into the lives and times of the Straits Chinese, the successive generations, their livelihood, public services, recreation and festivities.

Although Song Ong Siang was a much respected community leader, he was not wholeheartedly accepted by the conservative elements within the Chinese community, who found him too westernised.

Song Ong Siang was the founding President of the Old Rafflesians' Association. It was most appropriate that one of its famous old boys should be conferred the special honour of heading it.

A Farewell to Arms

Su Guaning

Su Guaning had always wanted to be an academic. Instead, he worked for 30 years as a Defence Scientist. Finally at fifty-two, he realised his ambition and became the second President of Nanyang Technological University in Singapore.

Su Guaning was born in Taiwan and came to Singapore at the age of seven. He studied at Nanyang Primary School, Catholic High School and Raffles Institution. Perceived as aloof by his friends because he often buried himself with books, he later decided to change his personality. He smiled more and became more outgoing.

A President's Scholar, he graduated in Electrical Engineering from Alberta University, obtained his Masters from the California Institute of Technology, and his doctorate from Stanford University.

Scholarly, bespectacled and soft-spoken, he hardly looked like a War Hawk. Yet he had spent 30 years purchasing and adopting military weapons for Singapore, including F16 fighter aircraft, guns, rifles, submarines and explosives. He joined the Defence sector soon after his graduation in 1972. Prior to becoming the President of NTU, he was the Chief Executive of the Defence Science and Technology Agency.

For Su, it was a case of being third time lucky when he joined NTU, as he could not be released because of his Defence expertise. He was selected after a worldwide search which evaluated 150 names to find a suitable person. His impressive scholastic record, on top of his experience in R&D, as well as in managing large organisations gave him the edge over others. He had been a Council member and being bilingual, he could also win the support of former Nantah graduates.

Su believes that he has found the commonality in managing a tertiary institution and a technological Defence outfit. "It is all about people. Universities can play a major role in supporting industry, as they train staff with highly specialised skills for the research and development field." He also recalls that Defence work was clouded in secrecy in the early days. "I could not even tell people where I actually worked."

His exposure abroad has helped him to shape his liberal views on managing people. "You have to treat humans as humans, not as machines. It's the job of management to create the right kind of environment for them to excel."

Su heads the NTU with its 2,000 academic staff and 24,000 undergraduates. He is given the challenging task of guiding NTU to its next stage of development. "What I want is essentially to turn out from NTU, a generation of Singaporeans who will be equally at home, dealing with Americans in Silicon Valley and also with people in China, with their historical and cultural heritage. If Singaporeans do not have that in them, Singapore will be bypassed. We should also give the students the incentive to strive for themselves, rather than giving it all to them on a silver platter. There is also a lot more energy among the students, in terms of their voice in university matters."

Su Guaning had to wait 30 years before he kept his tryst with his first love — academia. He is determined to transform NTU into a comprehensive university and to take it to a higher peak.

The Play's the Thing

Leaena Tambyah

Leaena Tambyah *nee* Chelliah, qualified as a professional social worker. However, she has devoted the greater part of her life to voluntary service, especially for children and young adults with special needs. Under her inspiring leadership of more than 30 years, the Asian Women's Welfare Association's (AWWA's) General Welfare Services, grew to be the forerunner of Singapore's Family Service Centres. She is best known for her pioneering work in caring for, and starting Singapore's first school for children with multiple disabilities in 1979. Leaena also introduced a mobile therapy service for students with physical disabilities in mainstream education, whose parents could not afford the money or the time to take their children to hospitals for therapy. This is a feature of AWWA's Therapy and Education for Children in Mainstream Education or TEACH ME Services. Raffles Girls' Secondary School became the first school in Singapore to become completely disabled-friendly for students with physical disabilities.

At an early age, she was exposed to the plight of the underprivileged. "My parents were very much involved in community service and I often accompanied them when they visited the hospitals and homes run by voluntary welfare organizations (VWOs)." Her father, Ven Dr D. D. Chelliah, was an educationist and the first Asian Archdeacon of St Andrew's Cathedral.

The enlightened family environment fired her ambition to be a professional social worker. At that time, the local university only offered a diploma course and the minimum age for admission was 26 and she was too young. So she proceeded to Birmingham University in England. After her graduation, she worked as an Assistant Director with the Department of Social Welfare. Subsequently, she resigned when she and her husband started their family and she wanted to care for their children herself.

She received her primary and secondary education at RGS and joined the Post School Certificate Arts class in Raffles Institution in 1955. In 1956, Leaena became the first female student at RI to join the Prefectorial Board.

It is with the Asian Women's Welfare Association that Leaena Tambyah is acknowledged for her pioneering work. A volunteer for more than 30 years, she is currently their Advisor. "It has given me many opportunities and much fulfilment, working with children and young people with special needs." She is the author of *Three Special Friends,* a children's book which is her personal tribute to them. Her good friend, Mrs Kathleen Chia, did the one-liners for pre-schoolers as well as the poem dedicated to special children. The artist Hiroko Miyamoto, another good friend, illustrated the stories. Leaena also edited *Hey Listen! We Have Something to Say!,* a collection of heart-warming stories written by young people who are part of AWWA's TEACH ME Services.

AWWA, whose philosophy is that every single person is important, is now a leading voluntary welfare organisation in Singapore. Leaena fully deserves the numerous awards for her community service. She was voted 'Woman of the Year' in 1994.

She has achieved much, with the understanding and support of her husband, John Tambyah who is a consultant endocrinologist. They first met when they were drawn together by their common interest in drama and John was the Secretary and Leaena the Chairman of *The Raffles Players.* While Leaena was reciting her lines on stage as Maria in *Twelfth Night,* John was busy behind the scenes, occupied with the stage management and the printing of the concert programmes on the Gestetner duplicator. Their romance blossomed. They have a son and a daughter and three grandsons.

She was in the habit of taking off her shoes in class, to feel more comfortable. One day, when the bell rang for school dismissal, she could not find one of her shoes. Someone had stolen it from under her feet. Like Cinderella, it had a happy ending — Leaena had lost her shoe and found her Prince Charming in John Tambyah.

Taking the Nation's Pulse

Tan Cheng Bock

Tan Cheng Bock has been the most prominent government backbencher for the past 25 years. He is highly regarded by Members of Parliament for his forthright views, sincerity and humility. Speaking without fear or favour, he has occasionally incurred the wrath of ministers. In his dual role as doctor and politician, he is eminently qualified to feel the pulse of Singaporeans.

He studied at Radin Mas Primary School and, from 1955 to 1960, at Raffles Institution, where he developed his leadership qualities as a Boy Scout. He graduated in Medicine from the University of Singapore in 1968. The third of eight children, he lost his father when he was fourteen. It was a hard struggle for him to pay his university tuition fees.

As a young doctor in 1968, Tan Cheng Bock opened his zinc-roofed wooden clinic in Lim Chu Kang. Although Medicine was his first love, he soon realised that he had another calling — politics. His patients were mostly farmers and, in addition to attending to their health, he had to petition to the authorities about their socio-economic problems ranging from illegal squatting, education and family disputes. Although it was clear to him that he could do more in politics, he thought he should first establish his career.

It was in 1980 that he was initiated into politics by his lifelong friend and classmate, Goh Chok Tong. "I entered politics because I wanted to make a contribution to my country. Twenty-five years ago, Singapore was in the midst of transition from a Third World country. Old guards were stepping down and new ones had to be found to replace them.

I belong to that early political renewal change and I quickly found a role in the House, hoping to bring about changes in the country. There were no Opposition members in Parliament at the time and I found myself inevitably playing the role of checking the front bench policymakers. In the early 80s, changes in education, particularly those related to streaming, caught my attention. My concern was that streaming would stratify our society and develop class divisions. My bluntness angered the then Education Minister."

In 1985, he was appointed the first Chairman of the Feedback Unit. "Most people expect all their views to be accepted and action taken. If not, they think that you are not listening to them. Feedback is for the sharing of ideas. It is not for you to impose your ideas on me and *vice versa*. My main concern is how to get across to the powers-that-be, the people's deep feelings on various issues. I tell them to the ministers. But one element is missing. I cannot express their emotions and fears. It is up to the ministers to go down to the ground and pick up those feelings themselves." His colleagues agree that Cheng Bock is a good listener who has a very concerned look on his face when he is listening to others. He always says that we must take the side of the people. His favourite phrase is "I'm prepared to err on the side of the people."

Cheng Bock has held his seat in the Ayer Rajah Constituency since 1980. In 2001, he was returned with a massive 88 percent majority vote. An outspoken but loyal backbencher, he was a critic of two important government policies. In 1992, he was against the appointment of Nominated Members of Parliament. "I was against this, because I believe that MPs must be elected by the people and be accountable for their actions. I voted against my Party. Also, my call to think 'Singaporeans first' during the debate on foreign talent was rebutted very strongly by the ministers. I was even accused of being anti-national."

Cynics might call him a rebel, but Tan Cheng Bock is certainly a rebel with a cause. His contributions have been recognised by the People's Action Party. He was the only backbencher to be elected into its Central Executive Committee. He was also the Coordinating Chairman of all the Government Parliamentary Committees. He has also served as the Chairman of the Education, National Development and Environment GPCs, Town Councils and Community Development Councils.

He was instrumental in securing from the government the use of the Central Provident Fund for tertiary education, and the implementation of free parking on HDB estates on public holidays.

In his dual role as a doctor and a politician, Tan Cheng Bock is a backbencher who takes the nation's pulse. He is an indispensable link between the government and the people.

Father of the Malayan Chinese

Tan Cheng Lock

Tan Cheng Lock is one of the greatest and best known of Malayan leaders. Called 'The Sage of Malacca', he championed many reforms for the Chinese community. As one of the architects of Malayan Independence, he has earned his niche in Malayan history.

He was born in Malacca in 1883. His grandfather pioneered the tapioca and gambier plantation industry and also founded the Straits Steamship. Tan Cheng Lock received his education at the Malacca High School and Raffles Institution where he taught for six years. He later returned to his home town and became a rubber planter. He also had considerable business interests, including banking, shipping and a newspaper. In British Malaya, his wealth and Western liberal education were his great assets.

Tan was initiated into public service in 1912, when he was appointed a Justice of the Peace. He was a Legislative Councillor for many years and as an accomplished speaker, he was known as 'The Silver Tongue Orator'. A 'King's Chinese', he served as a private in the Chinese Volunteer Corps. During the First World War, he led fund-raising campaigns, which included the presentation of an aeroplane to the British government.

He zealously fought for Chinese marriage reform, advocated the opening of agriculture schools, and displayed a special interest in technical education. Although he had wide knowledge of Chinese history and culture, he was also steeped in Western philosophy and drew inspiration from Plato. It was little wonder he was called 'The Sage of Malacca'. For his public service and for supporting inter-communal cooperation, he was knighted and awarded the CBE.

Tan was a living example of the concept 'Malayan'. Although he took pride in Chinese culture and tradition, his first loyalty was to the land of his birth, and in 1928, he advocated the forging of a Malayan nation with complete elimination of racial and communal sentiments. He had envisaged a British Malaya, not knowing that within the next 30 years, Malaya would attain Independence.

In 1949, Tan Cheng Lock became the founding President of the Malayan Chinese Association, a move which coincided with the rising political consciousness of the Chinese population. However, the English-speaking Tan Cheng Lock made little impact on the masses, especially with the extremist elements. While addressing a rally, he was wounded by a hand grenade thrown at him by a terrorist.

Tan Cheng Lock's political legacy is that as the leader of the Malayan Chinese, he was one of the pillars of the UMNO-MCA-MIC Alliance which won Independence for Malaya in 1957. At the ripe old age of 76, he did not stand for election, preferring to remain as an elder statesman so the leadership of the MCA was assumed by his son, Tan Siew Sin, who later became the Malaysian Minister for Finance.

As a patriot, elder statesman and nation builder, Tan Cheng Lock was truly one of Malaysia's most illustrious sons.

Scholar and Olympian

Tan Eng Liang

Tan Eng Liang is Singapore's first Rhodes Scholar. While still in school, he represented Singapore in water polo at the 1956 Olympic Games in Melbourne. An outstanding sportsman all his life, he was the 'Supremo of Sports'. He was also a Corporate Chairman and a former Minister of State.

Eng Liang studied at Pasir Panjang Primary School and Raffles Institution from 1952 to 1957. He was a prefect and a swimming champion, specialising in the backstroke. He comes from a famous family of swimmers, which includes his brothers, Eng Bok and Eng Chai as well as his uncle Hwee Hock.

The young Eng Liang was thrown into the deep end when he represented Singapore in water polo at the 1956 Olympic Games at Melbourne. Rafflesians formed the core of the youthful team which was no match against the older and more experienced teams. However, Tan survived from this baptism of fire and was propelled into a lifetime commitment to swimming and sports. In the 1950s, Raffles reigned supreme in swimming. Its water polo team had gained such a fearsome reputation that no other school dared to take to the pool against it. Its invincible team of swimmers included Barry, Keith and Derek Mitchell, Voon Let Chai, Chan Thai Ho and Eric Yeo Oon Tat.

While keeping faith with his first love, Tan had to concentrate on his studies. He crowned his brilliant academic record by graduating with a First Class Honours in Chemistry from the then University of Malaya in Singapore in 1961. The next year, he was awarded a Rhodes Scholarship and he obtained his doctorate from Oxford University in

1964. This was no mean feat as this prestigious scholarship is awarded to those with academic as well as sporting excellence. Over the years, Rhodes Scholars have included many of the world's leaders, thinkers and intellectuals.

Tan Eng Liang holds directorships in several companies. Despite the heavy demands of the private sector, he still finds time for sports. He is the Vice-President of the Singapore National Olympic Council. It was *déjà vu* in 1984, when he was the *Chef de Mission* of Singapore's contingent to the Los Angeles Olympics. In his ten years as a participant, he had represented Singapore at the Tokyo and Bangkok Asian Games. When he was Chairman of the Singapore Sports Council in 1975, he brought about significant improvements in sports. He created the Sports Assistance Programme in which deserving sports people were each given $7,000 a year to help them strive for excellence in competition. "Despite our geographical and demographic size, Singapore should not be satisfied with being a country of mediocrity in sports. But money cannot buy commitment. The athletes must first show commitment before they ask for aid." Tan Eng Liang always believed in speaking his mind. He was also aware that the various associations are run by volunteers and that we cannot expect too much from them. He hoped that with funding and by employing full-time administrators, they would become more professional.

A very busy Corporate Chairman, his voluntary services are highly regarded by clubs and the community. He is on the Board of Governors of RI and the United World College. He is also a former President of the Singapore Island Country Club. His contribution to public service was recognised, when he became a Member of Parliament from 1972 to 1980, during which he served as Senior Minister of State (National Development) from 1975 to 1978 and as Senior Minister of State (Finance) from 1979 to 1980.

Tan Eng Liang has led a distinguished life, excelling in sports, scholarship, government, the corporate world and community service.

Fastest Man Wins

Tan Eng Yoon

Tan Eng Yoon was the fastest man in Singapore in the 1950s. He represented Singapore in the Olympic Games in Melbourne in 1956. He coached the post-War generation of national and international athletes. In a lifetime dedicated to athletics, he was a pioneer blazing the way as an Olympian, teacher, coach, author and administrator.

As a young boy he loved running. At the age of seven, he would climb over the ten-foot barbed wire gate of the Geylang Stadium and run barefoot round the field. He showed a clean pair of heels, whenever he was pursued by the *jaga*. He studied at Geylang English Primary School and was the school's champion athlete until 1940. "I won six out of the seven events. However, as a result of the exertions, I had jaundice and was banned by my father from taking part in sports activities."

In 1941, he was one of the top five students who were admitted to Raffles Institution. Tan's studies were interrupted by the Japanese Occupation and he did not return to school after 1945, but worked as a dental assistant in the RAF Dental Clinic. A teacher form St Joseph's Institution convinced him that he should resume his education and he completed his Senior Cambridge Examinations. "I was inspired by the religious brothers of the school and became a Catholic. I was almost disowned by my father."

As fate would have it, Tan's withdrawal from athletics was short-lived. By sheer chance, one evening he paced with the school's sprinter. His Housemaster noticed his potential and entered him for four events for the school sports. He won the 100, 220 and 880 yards events and was second in the long jump. His greatest triumph came in the inter-school sports. In the Mile Medley Relay, he ran the last leg of 880 yards, with the ACS rival already 100 yards ahead of him. To his great surprise and joy, he breasted the tape first. He became a Singapore champion sprinter at the age of 21, followed by similar triumphs in Malaya. For almost ten years, Tan was invincible, burning up the tracks. He was a natural athlete, at a time when there was virtually no proper coaching and training. His coach gave him Ovaltine to drink and plenty of rest before the events. But Tan did not rest on his laurels. He wanted to improve his performance and to raise the standard of athletics in Singapore.

His great opportunity came in 1955 when he was awarded a three-year scholarship to study Physical Education at Loughborough College, England. He was also awarded a German government scholarship to study sports organisations there. He is also a Master of Sports Science from the United States Sports Academy.

Tan Eng Yoon retired from international athletics in 1961. He had represented Singapore in two SEAP Games, two Asian Games, the Olympics in 1956 and the Commonwealth Games in Cardiff in 1958. He did not keep his many achievements to himself. Instead, he used his expertise in the performance of his public service. He was a Physical Education specialist in the Ministry of Education. He was also a lecturer at the Teachers' Training College. His other postings included Deputy Executive Director of the Singapore Sports Council, General Secretary of the Football Association of Singapore and President of the USA-ICSM programme. He has also published several authoritative books on athletics.

He established the National Training Squad to develop athletes with potential, coaching and training at all levels and specialist training centres.

He coached and inspired many national champions, including Rafflesian Evelyn Lee, who later became his wife. It was a happy ending to his illustrious athletic career. Tan Eng Yoon richly deserves his rightful place in the athletic and sporting annals of Singapore.

Water Polo Gold Medallist

Tan Hwee Hock

Tan Hwee Hock can be included in the select company of famous sportsmen who have won gold medals at international sports events. He achieved this remarkable feat when he represented Singapore in water polo at the 1954 Asian Games in the Philippines. He has devoted 55 years of his life to swimming and water polo as a national champion, lecturer, Physical Education specialist, administrator and technical adviser. A modest role model, he has coached and inspired many of our aquatic sportsmen, who have won national and international honours.

Hwee Hock was born in 1929 and attended Pasir Panjang Primary School from 1936 to 1941. He studied at Raffles Institution from 1946 to 1948, where he was the 3rd Raffles Troop Leader, shot-putt champion and judo enthusiast. Upon graduating from the Teachers' Training College, he was posted to Pasir Panjang Primary School, where he taught his top student, Goh Chok Tong. "He will always tell his friends that I was his teacher. He is a very humble and respectful person. I'm glad that he has done so well for himself. I also coached him in swimming and water polo."

Hwee Hock returned to RI as a teacher when he was offered the post by his old teacher, Mr V. Ambiavagar. In 1956, he was awarded a scholarship to study Physical Education at Loughborough College. A specialist in Physical Education, he lectured at the National Institute of Education and the College of Physical Education. From 1963 to 1984, he was an Assistant Inspector of Schools.

Hwee Hock was the national breaststroke champion in 1949. He hails from a family of swimmers which includes his elder brother, Wee Chwee, who was the national champion before the War. Swimming came to him naturally as their home was in Pasir Panjang, which means 'Long Beach'. He learned to play water polo in the Tiger Swimming Club, a club which has spawned many national champions. "We became a formidable team, because we often played with teams from the British forces. Our members formed the nucleus of the Singapore team which won a silver medal at the first Asian Games in New Delhi in 1951. Our swimming team also won a silver medal. I swam the butterfly leg in the medley."

The year 1954 saw his greatest triumph at the Asian Games in Manila when he struck gold. Against all odds, Singapore defeated Japan 4-2 in the finals. "I scored three goals, two with the back throw. I was eight metres from the goalpost and I caught the Japanese goalkeeper by surprise, because my back was towards him and he never expected me to score from that position. We had started as the underdogs. We won because we played as a team and every member was pumped up to bring glory to Singapore. Our famous victory inspired a new generation of youngsters to learn the game and to have the honour of representing Singapore. Before this, water polo was a relatively unknown game played only by a few diehards."

He had set his sights on the 1956 Olympic Games in Melbourne as he had assumed the captaincy of the Singapore team. However, at the same time, he had been awarded a departmental scholarship to study Physical Education at Loughborough College. "I was faced with a dilemma. Should I seize the golden opportunity to further my career prospects, or should I go to the Olympics? In the end, it was Hobson's choice. My career had to come first." Nevertheless, his love for water polo did not leave him. When he was in England, he became the only Asian in the British universities team.

Hwee Hock regrets that Singapore has never recaptured the glory of 1954. "We have invariably finished third or fourth in the Asian Games. This is because water polo is an amateur's game, unlike in some countries where it enjoys a quasi-professional status. We have been SEA Games champions all these years. Even here, we are under threat by other neighbours who have invested heavily in training and facilities.

We have the talent, but are our youngsters prepared to sacrifice their time for training and to risk their employment prospects?"

Throughout his long educational career and as the Vice-President of the Singapore Swimming Association, Tan Hwee Hock has fervently promoted the cause of swimming and water polo, for which he is truly a pioneer in his own right. Our aquatic sportsmen owe him a debt of gratitude for blazing the trail in the swimming pool and for bringing glory to Singapore.

Chess Prodigy

Tan Lian Ann

The name of Tan Lian Ann ranks second only to Lim Kok Ann in the game of chess in Singapore. A chess prodigy and an international Chess Master, he reigned supreme in the 1950s and 60s as the Singapore and Malayan Chess Champion. He also scored phenomenal successes in international tournaments. In one epic encounter, he drew his match with Boris Spassky, the world champion.

Tan studied at Winstedt Primary School and received his secondary education at RI, completing his 'A' levels in 1963. He is an Accountancy graduate of the University of Singapore. He obtained his Masters of Business Administration from NTU at the age of 47. After working as an accountant in several international firms, he became an entrepreneur dealing in German stationery. Currently, he deals in toys and baby products, with Indonesia as his main market.

Lian Ann was drawn to the game of chess at the age of eight. His father gave him ten cents for every game that he won against him. He and his brothers, Lian Quee and Lian Seng, kept the Singapore Schoolboy Championship within the Tan family for five years, from 1957 to 1961. The Raffles chess team was invincible against other schools and its members also beat older opponents, including university professors. In 1960, he captained the Singapore Goodwill Team to Malaya to compete against student and adult clubs. At the age of 14, he became the Malayan champion, taking only six hours to defeat the older reigning champion.

Lian Ann was the first Singaporean to be conferred the title of 'International Chess Master'. He was given the coveted award by the World Chess Federation (FIDE) for reaching the quarter-finals of the world championships. His record is phenomenal. As a teenager, he had already defeated much older chessmen in international tournaments. He has chalked up 12 Malayan championships since 1958. He was fourth in the World Junior Championships.

One of his most memorable moments came in 1963, when he came in second in the Australian Open. The Finance Minister then, Dr Goh Keng Swee, was very impressed by his sterling performance. He ensured that the 15-year-old Lian Ann was given a hero's welcome on his return. It was a proud day for him when he was driven away from Kallang Airport in a motorcade, with Dr Goh seated beside him. It was a touching tribute by Dr Goh, who was himself a reputable chessman. Another highlight of his illustrious record was when the 25-year-old Lian Ann took on the 45-year-old world champion, Boris Spassky. Their five-hour epic encounter ended in a draw.

Lian Ann attributes his passion for chess and his prodigious achievements to Prof Lim Kok Ann, who coached him since he was ten. "Prof Lim was my mentor. He was more like a father to me. He gave me chess sets and books. He also encouraged me in my studies. His advice was always "Eat first". He constantly stressed that I should get a degree and not devote most of my time to chess." Lian Ann has coached many young chess players who later became National Masters. When he was twelve, he taught students in the School for the Blind. "It was a most gratifying and meaningful experience. Several of them were so good that they were able to play chess, without using the board. They have also competed in national tournaments, much to the chagrin of the sighted chessmen, should they lose to them."

He believes that chess is still very relevant today, the advent of information technology notwithstanding. "It's good training for the mind and helps you to concentrate. It has helped me in my business as I calculate, not just by numbers, but also, by thinking of tangibles and intangibles. I also do not act on impulse. So I strongly recommend that Singaporeans regard the game of chess as part of life. One good thing is that it disciplines you. When you play for four hours, you have no time to do any mischief." He feels that this could keep the restless youngsters off the streets, particularly, the drug addicts.

Lian Ann advocates that our youngsters should have a stint of chess, so that they can have a recreation that develops their powers of concentration. But it should not be at the expense of jeopardising their studies and employment prospects. "Naturally, they need not go as far as the way I went. I skipped classes in school and in the university to compete in tournaments. Today, they cannot afford to do that because of the priorities in our educational system."

Impacting Lives Beyond the Wheelchair

William Tan Kian Meng

He nearly had to live his life encased in an iron lung. He spent his childhood years crawling around. Called a 'crippled' boy, he was regarded good enough for a life in a sheltered workshop making handicrafts.

Dr William Tan rose above adversity. He became a legendary wheelchair marathon athlete and world famous fund-raiser. This 50-year-old paraplegic has completed 87 punishing marathons around the world, from Antarctica to Argentina, Thailand to USA to the North Pole, wheeling himself across deserts, mountain passes and icy terrains.

With 'eagle eye and gryphon strength', he has pushed boundaries. He proudly holds several world records for marathons. He has fund-raised over S$18 million for international charities over the last 20 years. The Global Flying Hospitals, Children Hospital Boston, Free Wheelchair Mission in California, Children with Leukaemia in London, St George Hospital in Sydney, Crippled Children Society in Auckland, Down Syndrome Association in Malaysia, Tan Tock Seng Hospital and National University of Singapore are just among some of the beneficiaries.

Born in 1957, William woke up one morning with high fever and vomiting at the age of two. When his legs buckled on trying to stand up, his parents realised the severity of his illness. He was kept in isolation for weeks at Middleton Hospital (known now as Communicable Disease Centre) where the doctors diagnosed him with poliomyelitis which paralysed him from the waist down. His parents were devastated that there is no cure for polio. Nevertheless, they refused to send him to the Red Cross Home for the Disabled. Against official advice in 1964, they chose to enrol him in mainstream schools to equip him with skills to face life's challenges with resilience and mental fortitude.

Fuelled by a desire to challenge his limitations, William topped Selegie Primary and went to Raffles Institution on a Ministry of Education Scholarship for his secondary and pre-university education. Many teachers had shaped his life including Captain Tan Kim Cheng and Dr Shirley Lim who gave him rides when RI moved from Bras Basah to Grange Road. William's father, who sold banana fritters along the streets, could no longer afford the transportation costs.

The National University of Singapore Alumnus who majored in Life Sciences joined the Civil Service after graduation in 1980. He ventured abroad for postgraduate studies in 1989. Holder of a First Class Honours in Physiology, this Harvard University's Fulbright Scholar and Oxford University's Raffles Scholar has also trained at the world-renowned Mayo Clinic in USA. Besides his career as a medical doctor and a neuroscientist, he also spends much time inspiring corporate executives and students round the world with stories from Antarctica, North Pole and from his life as a doctor on a wheelchair.

Wheelchair racing was introduced to him when he was sixteen by paraplegic sportsman, Wahid Baba. "When I sat in the wheelchair, I felt like a bird which had taken on a pair of wings. It was the first time that I sensed speed. I discovered how far I could go if I challenged myself." He was the first person to compete in a marathon on wheelchair in Singapore in 1980. Since then, he has never looked back.

William Tan has since achieved international fame with his Herculean marathons. Although he is regularly hitting the headlines with his monumental fund-raising efforts, he remains modest about his achievements. He attributed his success to effective synergy among his team members whose shared commitment is to maximise life and make a difference to humanity.

William Tan has contributed much more than his fair share to society. With his indomitable spirit, courage, perseverance and remarkable achievements, he is not only a role model to other disabled people, but also to all Singaporeans. He has shown by his inspiring example that disabled people should not be seen as passive recipients of charity and that they can also be contributing members of society.

He has certainly lived the vision of *'Auspicium Melioris Aevi'* and served by leading and being led by serving the community. A recipient of Harvard University's Albert Schweitzer (Nobel Laureate) Award, William has travelled a journey that "have been marked by a reverence for life and who has sought, as expressed by Schweitzer, to 'make my life my argument.'"

The Toy Piano

Margaret Leng Tan

Margaret Leng Tan has the unique distinction of being the first woman to graduate with a doctorate in music from Juilliard. She is one of those rare pianists whose performance style takes equal billing with the music, using sound, choreography and drama. Hailed as the world's premier prepared piano virtuoso and the diva *avant-garde* pianist, she is reputed for her performances of Asian and American music which defy the conventional boundaries of the instrument.

At Raffles Girls' School where she studied, her schoolmates recall a tiny figure with glasses and pigtails producing wonderful music from the piano to accompany the singing during school assemblies.

At sixteen, she won a scholarship to study at Juilliard and created history when she became the first woman to be conferred with a doctorate. She made her debut with the New York Philharmonic in 1991 playing John Cage's 1948 suite for toy piano. It was her tribute to her mentor who sparked her enchantment with the instrument. After falling in love with her first toy piano, she acquired many others, including a 37-key Schoenhut toy grand piano. "I remain wholeheartedly intrigued by the toy piano's magical overtones, hypnotic charm, and not least, its soft key poignancy."

Tan lives in Brooklyn, New York, with her two dogs, three Steinways and 12 toy pianos. She is closely identified with the works of John Cage and has captivated and enthralled audiences throughout the world with her unique performances. Her choreographic approach to the piano, reminiscent of Chinese *tai-chi,* is the outcome of finely coordinated movements between the keyboard and the piano's interior. In keeping with the philosophy of her mentor, John Cage, Margaret Leng Tan's performances combine an Eastern spiritual concentration, the Zen art of non-doing, with her Western classical training. This is evident, whether she is playing the keyboard on the strings of the piano, or even as she enters the world of her toy piano. Her intense commitment to her art is unwavering.

Tan made history again when she became the first Singaporean musician to play in the Carnegie Hall's Isaac Stern Auditorium. The 2,800-seat theatre is the largest of three performing spaces at the compound. "It is by doing something outlandish that you get to play there. If you think of Carnegie Hall, you think of it as a very traditional place. It is wonderful that they have made such forays into new music. Cage today isn't as outlandish as he once was. He has become a respected figure. That's why the Establishment is paying attention."

For her performance, she inserts the standard hardware stuff of screws, plastic, felt, bamboo and rubber into the piano body. The process alters the tone production mechanism of 53 different notes on the piano, so that the instrument twangs with a huge variety of sounds. This is required in many of John Cage's famous pieces in which she specialises. "It took me two days to put in all the stuff. It is really quite a complicated process. Life is full of ironies." Margaret Leng Tan muses over the reverse route she has taken by making her name before making her debut at the Hall. Most others treat the venue as a career launch pad, whereby a concert makes or breaks a musician.

Although Margaret Leng Tan is now an American citizen, Singapore is indeed proud that one of her daughters has become a superstar in her unique niche in the world of music.

PWD Director-General

Tan Swan Beng

Tan Swan Beng was an engineer with a strong passion for engineering excellence and innovation. He was a champion of technology. He was undoubtedly an engineer of great distinction who reached the pinnacle of his profession as Director-General of the Public Works Department. His lifelong work encompassed his considerable contribution to the construction industry, academia and civil aviation.

He was the eldest child of a sailor and a housewife. He was born in 1939 and educated at Winstedt Primary and Raffles Institution from 1954 to 1959. A brilliant scholar, he topped the 1957 Cambridge School Certificate Examinations for the whole of Singapore by scoring eight distinctions. He was a State Scholar and graduated from the University of Malaya with First Class Honours in Civil Engineering. He then proceeded on a Commonwealth Scholarship to the prestigious Imperial College, where he obtained his Masters and PhD in Soil Foundation.

Tan was always generous with his advice in RI and unselfishly tutored his friends. He would tell them, "Go back to basics. Memory can fail you, but if you remember the basics, you'll be fine." He was also very determined and persistent. If he believed in something, nothing could sway him. His classmates described him as "humble, honest and brilliant."

He joined the Public Works Department in 1968 and became its Director-General in 1986, a post he held until his death in 1998. His staff held him with respect and awe and remember him as a leader with strong convictions, a sharp mind and with a deep passion for engineering excellence and innovation. Under his dynamic leadership, the PWD established the reputation as an engineering authority with uncompromising standards for professional integrity in Singapore. He was directly responsible for the numerous major projects, including the development of Changi International Airport and the transformation of the road infrastructure in Singapore into one of the safest and most efficient road systems in Asia, the Benjamin Sheares Bridge, Singapore's first underground road, the Central Expressway; and the computerised area traffic control, the Malaysia–Singapore second causeway, and Revenue House. He also played a major role in making amendments to the Building Control Act to ensure safe and sound buildings. A specialist in geotechnical engineering, he contributed significantly to research and education, publishing 50 papers in international journals as well as authoring the book *The Geology of Singapore.*

As the Adjunct Professor and Council member of the Nanyang Technological University, Tan Swan Beng provided invaluable expertise to the overall development of the university, particularly in the areas of applied research development, staff establishment, and planning and development of building infrastructure on the campus. He was instrumental in the establishment of the Centre for Transportation, which was aimed at supporting Singapore's strategic development as an international hub for land, air and sea transportation. As President of the Institute of Engineers, he raised the professional standards of training and education of engineers.

Tan Swan Beng died in 1998 at the age of 58 of liver cancer. A consummate professional, he was working right to the very end. His friends remember him as an essentially private family man, who dressed simply and who preferred eating at hawker centres rather than restaurants. He often told them that his work as an engineer was to make life better for the community. In recognition of his distinguished public service and outstanding achievements, NTU created the Tan Swan Beng Professorship. It was initiated by his classmates and enthusiastically supported by members of the profession, industry and the government.

As its Director-General for 12 years, Tan Swan Beng had taken on the formidable task of transforming the Public Works Department into one of the best in the world. The many excellent public works in Singapore bear testimony to his legacy.

Poker King of Europe

Willie Tann Boon Guan

Willie Tann Boon Guan did not walk the conventional and well trodden paths of life. He studied Law, but became a professional gambler instead. In his 45 years of playing poker, he has seen the game evolve from being played in seedy basements and smoky halls to more salubrious surroundings and prestigious venues. He is the 2005 winner of the coveted World Series of Poker 18-Carat Gold Bracelet. He gives lessons to millionaires and celebrities.

The young Willie Tann studied at Outram Primary School and at Raffles Institution from 1955 to 1957. He read Law at the University of Singapore and Lincoln's Inn. At Raffles, he was a model student and holder of the Green Cord of the 32nd Scout Troop. He also represented Raffles and the Combined Schools at rugby. "Raffles has prepared me for life. There were ten of us. We spent our childhood together, practically every weekend. Our friendship has lasted through the years. Goh Chok Tong is still very humble and modest. He advises me to save for a rainy day."

Willie's life took an unexpected turn when he entered the University of Singapore. "I started playing poker and going to the races. I skipped lectures. I only started gambling when I was in varsity. It caused my downfall," he recalls laughingly. He had hoped that when he read Law at Lincoln's Inn, he would be able to kick the habit. "I played poker with my fellow students and I was winning a lot of money. So I stopped playing with them and started playing in Spielers and casinos all over London. I had part-time jobs, including that of a croupier. I thought that I could make a better living in poker. I had been in other businesses, such as being a restaurateur and bookmaker. But poker has always kept me going."

Far from being the urban casino dweller, Willie Tann lives some distance out of London, in a small village in Hertfordshire, where Tudor houses, churches and greenery are more common than casinos. Away from poker, he also has a family. "I have been married for almost 30 years now and I have a son. He went to Westminister and Oxford and is now a lawyer."

Nicknamed Mr Miyagi of 'The Karate Kid' fame, Willie Tann has been at the forefront of European poker for many years. He attained the pinnacle of his many achievements in 2005, when he walked away with the coveted World Series of Poker 18-Carat Gold Bracelet sponsored by Bet Fair Poker, ploughing his way to victory through the field of 743 to win $186,000. He is acknowledged as a true gentlemen on and off the table and a phenomenal poker player. He is a very friendly and amiable person who brings humour and good fun to any table he sits at. He shares the experience of one who has seen one million Hands. "Poker should be recognised as a sport, as there is a lot of skill involved besides the luck factor. There are so many ways of playing a Hand. No one can teach you to play a certain Hand in a certain way." The cornerstone of his teaching is the 5 P's: Patience, Perseverance, Psychology, Practice and Position.

He predicts that poker will eventually become as fashionable as bridge. Similarly, poker may come to be regarded, like *mahjong*, as a form of entertainment, no longer classified as gambling. "People think very positively of a poker player now. Every American whiz kid aspires to be a World Poker Champion. Nowadays, poker is played in salubrious surroundings and not in seedy, smoky joints."

Willie Tann expresses his concern for the young who take to gambling. "My best advice to them is to do their studies first so that they will have something to fall back on. I have known students who have given up their studies to play poker professionally, but I will strongly advise against it. They think it's so glamorous and so easy to make money from gambling."

Willie Tann, the professional gambler for 45 years and the Poker King of Europe has the last word on gambling. "Gamblers get into trouble sometimes. Gambling is alright, if it's kept under control. If you don't control gambling, it can ruin your life. You should only gamble within your means. People gamble because they think it's one of the quickest and easiest ways to get rich but you can be addicted to it, just like drugs."

The Speaker Speaks Out

Abdullah Tarmugi

Abdullah Tarmugi was a Shakespearean actor when he was a student. As a journalist, government minister and Speaker of Parliament, he has had his fair share of real life drama.

He attended Monk's Hill Primary School and Raffles Institution from 1959 to 1964. In RI, Abdullah Tarmugi was a prefect and also an actor, playing the role of Mark Anthony. He also represented RI in rugby. He graduated from the University of Singapore with a degree in Social Science.

He was a civil servant, journalist and Research Manager before his election as the Member of Parliament for the Siglap Constituency in 1984. He was the Minister for Community Development in 1994 and Minister in charge of Muslim Affairs. He was appointed the Speaker of Parliament in 2000.

As the Minister in charge of Muslim Affairs, Tarmugi occupied a hot seat. As the chief Malay-Muslim leader, he had to speak up for his Constituency. In 1999, the government's plan to introduce compulsory primary education caused controversy. Some Muslims feared the demise of the *madrasahs*, which groomed students to become Islamic scholars and teachers. Also, the Association of Muslim Professionals had proposed a collective leadership of independent Malay-Muslim leaders, which was rejected by the Cabinet. Another issue was whether girls should be allowed to wear the *tudung* or Islamic head scarf in national schools.

As Community Development Minister, he paid special attention to the problems of a rapidly ageing population and to the family and also drew up the blueprint for sports. He describes his years in the Cabinet as enriching and fulfilling. "It is very satisfying to know that you have contributed at that level. Not many have the privilege of doing so. So I'm quite thankful." In 2002 at the age of 57, he was appointed as Speaker of Parliament.

He defines the modern Malay as one who is broad-minded and rational, who thinks with his head and not with his heart. He acknowledges that in their quest for progress, the attitudes of the Malays have changed, but they still have to overcome the minority group syndrome, which gives rise to insecurity and over-sensitivity. He adds that Malays should view themselves from the national perspective. Only then can they realise the challenges faced by Singaporeans. The key challenge for Malays is the need to concentrate on education and to prepare themselves for the knowledge economy.

Tarmugi is keenly aware of the importance of global Islam. It is very difficult for Muslims living in a multiracial society to run away from it. He asserts that most Malay Singaporeans are moderate who make up the silent majority living in the HDB heartland and are not easily influenced by extremist elements. The emotional pulls of Indonesia and Malaysia are also decreasing, especially among the young.

How does Abdullah Tarmugi feel to be a Rafflesian holding such a highly esteemed post as Speaker of Parliament in Singapore? Of this, he says, "It has been more than 50 years. But the pride of being an alumnus of a famous institution still remains. The years spent in RI were among the happiest and most meaningful in my life. I had an education in the fullest sense of the word as I learned from my teacher and friends. The school provided me with learning opportunities and a social environment which I could not have had in any other school. Being a Rafflesian, I somehow had to live up to the school's expectations and use my achievement to serve others. RI moulded me into the person that I am today."

Law Professor and Human Rights Champion

Alice Tay Erh Soon

Alice Tay Erh Soon left Singapore when she was twenty-seven and settled in Australia, where she became a Law Professor and a champion of human rights. In her lifetime, she was showered with many honorific epithets, including that of "an absolute dynamo, huge intellect, not afraid to go into battle and *femme fatale*."

Tay, born in 1934, succumbed to lung cancer at the age of 70. She studied at Raffles Girls' School, where she was a brilliant student and completed her Senior Cambridge Examinations in 1952. Her parents, who owned a shoe store, bowed to her ambition to be a lawyer. She passed her Bar examinations at Lincoln's Inn in 18 months.

"On the first day of my return to Singapore, I went to see David Marshall. That took a lot of cheek because I had no connections. He paid me $250 a month. I gave my father $100, kept $50 for myself and paid off the piano with the other $100." After two years, she became an assistant lecturer in Law at the University of Malaya, then located in Singapore, where she inspired the pioneering batch of Law students with her beauty and intellect.

The projectory of her life was altered by the arrival of Eugene Karmenka, a German Jew who taught Logic at the Philosophy Department. They were inseparable and, after a tempestuous love affair, left Singapore to teach at the Australian National University in Canberra. They married in 1964. It was a defining alliance as Karmenka was one of the most respected thinkers in Australian intellectual life. The couple was the toast of the campus. "I don't like wishy-washiness. I don't like pale ghosts. I like people who are engaged, people with *gravitas.* When I started on a path, I take it to the end." She described her nine years at the ANU as difficult. A young Asian woman with a PhD had little in common with her faculty colleagues, which included the ritual of beer-drinking with the boys after lectures. Tay concentrated on scholarship and through sheer intellectual will, she mastered the original texts of Norman French and Russian. She was also fluent in Mandarin.

Weighing barely 40 kg, her small frame contained a large intellect. As a senior academic, she railed against declining standards. The university, she asserted, had become comfortable with the superficial, the fashionable and the shallow. Typical was this sort of exchange:

Tay: For our universities to become corporatised — money-making operations, is a recipe for dishonesty and hypocrisy.

Q: What about the Harvard model, a private university with enormous wealth and prestige?

Tay: Harvard, don't talk to me about Harvard. I wouldn't send my enemy's children to Harvard.

After the government appointed her to the Chairmanship of the Human Rights and Equal Opportunities Commission, she criticised its refugee policy, especially the detention of children. "Contrary to appearance, meek and mild as I may seem, I have been screaming the last few years." Her resumé only suggests the breadth of her intellectual life: PhD, ANU; Member of the Order of Australia; Challis Professor of Jurisprudence of the University of Sydney for 26 years; Fellow of the Australian Academy of Social Sciences; and other international accolades.

As Professor of Jurisprudence, she fought tooth and nail to prevent her Department from being merged with the Law Faculty. This battle reflected her own move away from the mere teaching and practice of Common Law to other fields, including Comparative Law, Legal Philosophy, and the History of Ideas and Human Rights. This is reflected in her scholarly books, monograms, articles and government reports.

Tay was notoriously active. She set up the Centre of Asian-Pacific Law to tap into the growing linkages between Australia and Asia, after the collapse of the Soviet system. It offered off-shore degree courses in China and Vietnam.

In 2004 and at the age of 70, Alice Tay Erh Soon succumbed to lung cancer. A fighter all her life for her own status and profession and for justice and human rights, she had fought her last battle.

Top Cop Held at Gunpoint

Tee Tua Ba

Tee Tua Ba was a Law graduate, but he did not practise Law. He was a crime and drug buster and Commissioner of Police. In his 30 years in the police force, his most terrifying moment was when he was held at gunpoint by a Red Brigade hijacker.

He was educated at Serangoon and Victoria School, and Raffles Institution. He graduated in Law from the University of Singapore in 1966 and was called to the Bar. However, he began his police career as a Cadet Assistant Superintendent of Police in 1967. He held various positions within the Ministry of Home Affairs before becoming Police Commissioner in 1992. These included Chief Instructor of the Police Academy, Director of the Central Narcotics Bureau (CNB), Deputy Commissioner of Operations, and Director of the Criminal Investigations Department (CID).

Tee's most memorable experience in his distinguished career was the role he played in the release of hostages, in the 1974 *Laju* incident. A group of Japanese Red Army and Palestinian terrorists had hijacked a Shell boat, after bombing an oil tank in Pulau Bukom. As Commander of the Marine Police, Tee was confronted with the awesome task of negotiating directly with the terrorists. "When one of them pointed a gun at me, I thought of my sons who were still very young. I was not sure that I would see them again. But I told myself that if I were to die, then, I wanted to die honourably, upholding the good name of the police force. So I told the terrorists that if they killed me, they would also be killed." Fortunately, the incident ended without bloodshed, with the exchange of civilian hostages for government officials who accompanied the terrorists on a plane to Kuwait.

As the CID Director, Tee did not believe in taking the soft approach towards crime. "We should not allow a small group of criminals to stop the vast majority of our people from enjoying a safe environment." Under his leadership, the crime rates were reduced and police-public cooperation was strengthened, chiefly with the introduction of the neighbourhood police force.

As Director of the CNB, he spearheaded 'Operation Ferret' which busted the drug trade. 'Black' areas, where the drugs were openly traded, were wiped out.

When Tee became the Director of Prisons, the prisons and drug rehabilitation centres were plagued with serious manpower shortage and overcrowding. He improved the morale and calibre of the officers with a revised scheme of service. New centres were set up to relieve over-congestion. New programmes for the treatment and rehabilitation of prisoners were also launched.

He played a leading role in initiating the building of the ultra-modern Tanah Merah Prison and Female Prison, and the Tampines Drug Rehabilitation Complex.

Tee Tua Ba retired from the Singapore Police Force in 1997 at the age of 55. He was appointed Ambassador to Brunei and, after that, as Ambassador to Egypt.

First Woman Olympian

Teng Pei Wah

Teng Pei Wah (or Tang Pui Wah) is Singapore's first woman Olympian. At the age of 19, she represented Singapore at the Helsinki Olympic Games in 1952. She competed in the 80-metres hurdles, in which she had been the undisputed Malayan champion for four consecutive years. She also won a bronze medal at the Asian Games in Manila in 1956.

Teng spent her early childhood in the congested Cross Street area of Chinatown. She attended Fairfield School in Neil Road during the War and was twelve when the Japanese Administration surrendered. She was active in school, often chasing the boys who teased her. Because of her educational abilities, she was admitted into Nanyang Girls' School and later, Raffles Girls' School.

Teng owes her athletic achievements to Nanyang Girls' School and the Singapore Chinese Amateur Athletic Federation. Nanyang had built up a fine sports tradition by importing teachers from China. The school was victorious in the Chinese Schools Combined Sports Meets, 1947–1949. Teng distinguished herself in the primary section, excelling in high jump and long jump, and as a hurdler and sprinter. Her height and speed propelled her to many victories in later years. "I was overage when I entered school, because of the War. I was in the primary section. The regular hurdler had left the secondary school. So I was asked to take her place."

Teng had been a shy and introverted young athlete, but she rapidly became a sporting legend in the 1950s. She was an instant sensation, soaring over the hurdles with seemingly effortless ease and grace.

The key to her success was her undoubted talent. She became the darling of the press in her late teenage years. The Singapore Chinese Amateur Athletic Federation also played a leading role in financing and promoting sports among the Chinese community. In 1947, Teng won her first major trophy in the high jump event organised by the SCAAF.

The turning point in her athletic career came, when she failed to qualify for the Malayan Chinese team to compete in Shanghai. "I wanted to be first." But she could only finish second in the high jump. "In those days, travelling was a wonderful thing. We looked towards China, not to the colony of Singapore. I didn't want to be second any more." Teng reigned supreme in the Singapore and Malayan athletic scenes, dominating the sprints and hurdles. She represented Singapore in the Asian Games in New Delhi in 1951.

Her greatest triumph came in 1952, when she became Singapore's first woman Olympian. She competed in the 100-metres sprint and 80-metres hurdles in Helsinki. The Singapore team consisted of Teng, three weightlifters, one swimmer and two officials. In Helsinki, the cold weather, the huge crowd, the unfamiliar track and lack of proper coaching weighed heavily against Teng.

Teng Pei Wah's burning ambition was to win an international medal. Her best chance came in 1954 when she represented Singapore in the Asian Games in Manila. She had entered for her pet event, the 80-metres hurdles. She was like a swan in flight, gliding over the hurdles, with her long legs and her ability to take only three instead of five steps between the hurdles. It was indeed her swan song and she felt that the gold medal was within her reach. Unfortunately, her hopes were dashed by an erratic start. Teng started slowly and had to be content with only a bronze medal. Although she still dominated the local scene, Teng had other priorities in mind, namely employment and marriage. So at the age of 22 she decided to retire from athletics.

Teng Pei Wah's achievements were formidable and inspiring, at a time when most girls fought shy of sports. She is a pioneer and role model for all aspiring sportswomen.

First Woman Pilot

Teo Ah Hong

Teo Ah Hong is Singapore's first female commercial pilot. With a commercial licence, she has trained many pilots who fly the Singapore International Airlines fleet. The name 'Hong' literally means 'Phoenix', so it seems that she was destined to fly.

Teo studied at Elling South Primary School and Raffles Girls' School from 1965 to 1971, where she obtained her 'A' levels. She is a Bachelor of Economics graduate of Sydney University.

She was one of the 17 schoolgirls who joined the Junior Flying Club in 1971. Her fascination for aeroplanes started when she was very young. "I could not resist looking up at the sky every time a plane flew by. I used to dream and wish that I could fly. As I grew older, I had the strong desire and the determination to become a pilot." After clocking about 250 hours of flying, she passed her examinations with flying colours and obtained her commercial pilot's licence in 1974, at the age of 22. "If every woman is given the opportunity to do a man's job, she will prove herself equally good, if not better." She also became the first female Singaporean instructor at the Singapore General Aviation Professional Pilots Training School. Although she had realised her dream to fly, she could not find employment as a pilot in the airlines. "When I went for interviews, they were very reluctant to let me have a chance to meet the interviewers. They also told me that if they had known that I was a female, they would not have called me."

Teo recalls her first flight in a Cessna 172. "Some 2,000 feet up, the earth below resembled a topographical map." For the next 30 years, she trained and tested pilots, culminating in her appointment as the Chief Flying Instructor of the Singapore Flying College (1990–2001). Thereafter, she spent another few years in aviation as a flying instructor of the Singapore Youth Flying Club.

Teo was responsible for the training of many SIA Captains and First Officers who piloted the A310, A340, B747 and B777 aircrafts. Ironically, she has flown full circle. She is bemused by the fact that her own ambition to be a SIA pilot was thwarted 30 years ago. Her colleagues and trainees speak highly of her professionalism and dedication to duty. She also acted as an authorised flight examiner. Teo always demanded the highest flying standards, thus ensuring the safety and comfort of SIA passengers. She thrived on work as well as being under pressure, whether in a team or unsupervised. She also has a sense of humour and exceptional culinary skills.

When I asked her if she ever had any anxious moments during her 30 years of flying, she laughed. “It happened in one of my first solo flights in a Cessna. I kept too close behind a bigger aircraft and was buffeted by its wake turbulence. I nearly plunged into the Straits of Johore.”

Teo Ah Hong’s success story is inspiring. “Friends’ discouragement of my flying only served to spur me on. The most important thing in life is always to think and act positive. Nothing is impossible in the long term. With determination and hard work, you will succeed and the world is a very fair place.” She speaks without rancour or bitterness when she reflects on how she had to overcome the prevailing prejudices and taboos.

Teo Ah Hong has found her niche in Singapore’s civil aviation industry. She dared to fly when flying as an occupation was considered hazardous, dangerous and unthinkable for a woman. A pioneer in flying, she has blazed the trail for other women to follow in her flight path.

National Library Chief

N. Varaprasad

N. Varaprasad (or Prasad) is best known as a progressive educator and educationist. His life has been predicated on the two pillars of public service and education, where he is highly regarded as an innovator and visionary. He was a lecturer, Associate Professor and later a Deputy President at the National University of Singapore. He was the founding Principal of Temasek Polytechnic. Now in his late fifties, as Chief Executive of the National Library Board, he is entrusted with the responsibility of keeping the national institution a key player in Singapore's drive to be a knowledge-based society, gracious, creative and engaged.

He was born in Rangoon, Burma, in 1948, coming to Singapore in early 1949. He attended Tanjong Rhu Primary School before going on to RI in 1961. "I grew up in Joo Chiat. The area had its fair share of haunted houses, ponds, ducks, fruit trees and open spaces. Like other kids of my generation, life was less about studies, and more on growing up. I remember pounding glass to reinforce kite strings, playing marbles and releasing paper boats in the monsoon drains when it rained. There were frequent gang fights on my street."

Prasad studied in Raffles from 1961 to 1966, and was active in the Army Cadets, reaching the rank of CSM. "My six years with RICC had the greatest influence on me, on my sense of loyalty and duty, and also on my punctuality, dress, decorum and respect for authority. We had the good fortune to be pushed hard. I attended the Outward Bound School at Lumut and the Jungle Warfare Training School at Ulu Tiram. At a young age, we were pushed to our physical limits and had the opportunity to shoot pistols and Bren guns and even throw grenades."

A Colombo Plan Scholar, he graduated in Engineering with Honours from the University of Canterbury and obtained his Masters in Engineering from the University of Auckland. Later in his career in 1980, he obtained his doctorate in Transport Studies from Cranfield, UK. He started his career as a lecturer in the Department of Industrial and Systems Engineering at the National University of Singapore, rising to the position of Associate Professor. He has published applied research papers in the areas of Transport and Urban Planning.

He entered Educational Management when he joined Singapore Polytechnic as Deputy Principal in 1985 and in 1990, was made founding Principal of Singapore's third polytechnic, Temasek Polytechnic, and serving for 11 years. As its Principal, he is credited with changing the image and profile of polytechnic education in Singapore as an attractive option for school-leavers.

He built up Temasek Polytechnic into a major institution with 13,000 students, in a colourful custom-built campus with the tagline 'Young, Bold and Caring', giving it a reputation for progressive educational methods, especially problem-based learning (PBL). He created new courses in Hospitality, Tourism, Law, Design, Retail Management, and Mechatronics, and introduced character education, inter-disciplinary studies and modular course structures. He also developed the idea of practice-based training by opening student-run travel agencies, retail outlets, and restaurants. When he was Deputy President of NUS, he was responsible for overseeing its corporate cluster of departments, including the library, computer centre, student affairs, arts and culture, occupational health and safety, and university health services.

Prasad explains why he joined the National Library Board as its Chief Executive this way. "It was mainly because I saw that this was an opportunity to go into education in a bigger way than anything I had done before, as the library is the key to stimulating lifelong learning among the broader population, not just students. Libraries connect people to knowledge useful for their total development at every stage of their lives, hence 'Libraries for Life, Knowledge for Success'."

"Libraries have played a transformative but largely unrecognised role in people's lives in deeply personal ways. The challenge is to keep the library relevant in the context of the digital revolution. Libraries are now at a very important inflexion point. The role of the librarian is also in flux as people have become more self-sufficient." Prasad categorically debunks the image of libraries as sedate throwbacks. "At the moment, the library is the most exciting place to be in, for we have to deal with real change. Libraries must complement rather than fight the Internet, by providing responsive 'just-in-time' trusted information."

Prasad has a clear vision for the development of libraries in Singapore. "Libraries may be said to perform six key roles — statutory, social, cultural, heritage, academic and economic. The economic role needs to be enhanced. Libraries need to have economic relevance, by delivering information to consumers, whether these be companies, policy makers or individuals, using multiple channels and technology. We have to be ever present not just in the digital space, but be present in every user's space. This is the challenge before us — to connect people to knowledge seamlessly, as well as connect people to communities of knowledge. The library of the future will become the switchboard connecting different knowledge communities, hence creating new insights, innovations and new knowledge by all."

Prasad has served on many public committees, community organisations and statutory boards such as STB, NHB, MRTC, HPB, and CSC. He was Deputy Chairman of the Action Committee on Indian Education and Vice-President of SINDA in its formative years. He chaired MOE's Tamil Language Pedagogy and Curriculum Review Committee. He is currently on the Board of Trustees of SIM University and the National Council Against Drug Abuse (NCADA). He is a recipient of the Public Administration (Gold) Award.

As the National Library Board's Chief Executive, we are confident that Prasad will take our library system, already one of the best in the world, to an even higher peak.

The People's President

Wee Kim Wee

Wee Kim Wee is affectionately known as 'The People's President' for bringing the highest Office of the nation to the man in the street. He is highly respected as a man without affectation and with a deep interest in people. He brought honour and dignity to the Presidency and his dedication to duty was exemplary.

He was a man of many parts, rising from clerk to reporter and Ambassador, and culminating his distinguished career in 1985 as Singapore's fourth President, an office he held for eight years. He collected stamps, coins, currency notes and handicrafts and listened to old Indonesian, Chinese and Western melodies.

He was born in 1915. At the age of six, he became the eyes of his 40-year-old blind father. His family moved to a house without electricity in Holland Road and reared poultry.

Wee started his education in Pearl's Hill School in 1923. He passed Standard 8 in RI and had to leave school at the age of 15 to support his widowed mother and grandparents.

In 1930, he got a job as a despatch clerk in the Circulation Department of *The Straits Times* with a monthly salary of $50. He moved up to advertising and reporting. In 1941, he joined the United Press International, an American news agency and became its regional correspondent and Manager. He rejoined *The Straits Times* in 1959 and worked his way up to the position of Editorial Manager. From 1973–1984, he was appointed a diplomat, representing Singapore in Malaysia, Japan and South Korea. He was the Chairman of the Singapore Broadcasting Corporation before he became Singapore's fourth President in 1985.

"When I first became President, the only thing on my mind was could I do my job to the satisfaction of those who put me in it? Every Singaporean has the right to have a people's President. You want someone who is approachable. So, there's nothing really amazing that the President of Singapore should be close to the people. At every official function, I wanted to meet as many people as possible. He had invited many public-spirited people to the Istana for tea and coffee and the First Lady's nonya cakes. Mrs Wee took her public role seriously and discharged it with warmth, grace and cheerfulness.

He remembers how he had gone through a very harsh life at school and at work. It gave him the feeling that he should be with the people and that he should not shun them. "When I attended my first few cocktails as a cub reporter, it was terrible. People won't even look at me. During colonial times, you have to have a big house and a Rolls Royce. Otherwise, you didn't matter at all. I was shunned bitterly. So, I told my staff, never allow the guests to be stranded. As President, if I don't make an effort to go down to the people, how will they come up? Any Singaporean can meet the President, if they want."

He regrets that Singaporeans have little time to think about helping those in need. "We push ourselves against the wall. We strive for excellence. There is very little time to ponder these subtleties and niceties." He also observes that today's children are born into a very good era with abundant opportunities. "When I was young, the furthest I went was Kota Tinggi on my bicycle. I left at 7 am and returned at 10 pm almost dead."

President Wee has led a very eventful and inspiring life, and he considers journalism the most interesting part of his career. Although as Singapore's High Commissioner, he played a vital role in consolidating ties with Malaysia, it was his eight years in the Istana which have given him the most satisfaction. He sums up his two terms as Singapore's President as satisfying, interesting, fascinating and illuminating. "I'm placed in a very strategic position, much more than any anybody else. I have a bird's eye view of what goes on in the region and also internationally."

President Wee Kim Wee retired at the age of 78 in 1993. For his outstanding service to the nation, he was conferred the Order of Temasek First Class.

He passed away on 2 May 2005 at the age of 89. Many Singaporeans wept when they paid their last respects to the people's President at the Istana. The Nanyang Techological University has named its communication school after him, calling it the Wee Kim Wee School of Communication and Information.

A Witness to End of Empire

Othman Wok

Haji Othman bin Wok has played a prominent role in Singapore's political development as a trade unionist, journalist, government minister and Ambassador. He has lived through British colonialism, the Japanese Occupation, Singapore's merger with Malaysia, its separation and eventual emergence as an independent nation. He was a keen sportsman in his student days, and when he was a government minister, sports was an integral part of his portfolio.

Othman Wok was educated at Telok Blangah Malay School, Radin Mas and Raffles Institution. He was a Scout and cadet. "I was an average student. I never thought that I could have achieved so much in my life. That's why I have entitled my autobiography *Never in My Wildest Dreams*."

He certainly could not have envisaged, how his life could be so eventful and colourful. Othman personally witnessed history in the making. On 8 December 1941, the Japanese forces invaded Kota Bahru and launched their Malayan campaign. "On that very same morning, I was sitting for my Senior Cambridge Examinations. It was a History paper and most of the questions were about the British Empire. The Hygiene paper was interrupted by a Japanese air raid and we had to run for shelter in the toilet. While waiting for the all-clear, we cheated and compared notes. The British soldiers guarding the school looked defeated and demoralised. The Japanese were bombing Singapore, causing heavy damage to British military installations and civilian lives. This was the first time that Singapore had experienced aerial bombing. The streets were clogged with people and their belongings, using cars, lorries, trishaws and bullock carts."

During the Japanese Occupation, Othman worked as a rat catcher transferring the fleas of dead rats into bottles. It was only after the War that he learned the Japanese had dropped them over Chungking, as a crude form of biological warfare. He also became a fisherman, refusing to be conscripted into the local army.

After the War, Othman join the *Utusan Melayu* as a reporter, with Yusof Ishak as its Editor. He was soon embroiled in trade union activities and was the Secretary of the Singapore Printing Employees Union. In the dispute between the Union and *The Straits Times*, he was threatened with arrest under the Emergency regulations. He was involved in the Malay version of *Petir* and the Malay Affairs Bureau. He was also the Chairman of the Geylang–Changi branch of the PAP. In the 1959 General Election, Othman narrowly lost to the UMNO candidate. In 1963, he was elected as the Member of Parliament of Pasir Panjang constituency. How did the PAP capture the Malay heartland of Geylang Serai and the Southern Islands from UMNO? "We gradually won their hearts and minds. We started *gotong royong* projects. We expanded on roads, street lights, water supply and other amenities for improving their livelihood."

As the Minister of Social Affairs, Othman was popular with his party colleagues and the people. His informality was reinforced by his previous experience as a trade unionist and journalist. After retiring from the government, he served as Singapore's Ambassador to Indonesia. He is also a retired Major in the People's Defence Force. This was *déjà vu*, a throwback to his schooldays in RI as a cadet.

The Consummate Journalist

Francis Wong Tze Kan

Francis Wong Tze Kan brought a refreshing change to journalism in Singapore. Hitherto, the Press was dominated by expatriates who wrote mainly for an English-educated readership who were sadly out of touch with the rapidly changing political events.

In RI, his talent for writing was very evident to his teachers and friends. He was the editor of *The Rafflesian.* Wong proceeded to Hong Kong to study Medicine, but his heart was not in it. His ambition was to be a journalist. At eighteen, he joined *The Straits Times* as a cub reporter in 1952. He quickly learned the ropes of journalism. Soon, he was hitting the by-lines. The police were looking for an armed criminal who walked with a limp. Francis Wong had a brilliant idea. Wearing dark glasses, his trousers bulging with an improvised pistol, he deliberately limped into a police station, pretending to ask for street directions. The policemen were not impressed and sent him on his way. He also approached several passengers at a bus stop, but no one paid him any attention. The press photographer who accompanied him, took pictures of his encounters. This was one of the many scoops which propelled Francis Wong into journalistic prominence.

His rise was meteoric and he was promoted to the job of Editor of the *Sunday Mail* at the relatively young age of 26. He was awarded the Nieman Scholarship to study Journalism at Harvard. The *Sunday Mail* was the hallmark of his talent, excelling in journalistic, photographic and technical standards. With its liberal image, the weekly newspaper struck an immediate chord with a new generation of intellectuals, who found it uniquely refreshing and stimulating. Wong had broken the mould of a traditionally conservative colonial press, which had been dominated by expatriates.

Bespectacled, with his boyish demeanour, Wong was always seen sporting a cravat and smoking a cigarette with a holder. He was a giant among his colleagues. As President of the National Union of Journalists, he was popular and respected for his professionalism. He read extensively and often alluded to the works of George Bernard Shaw and Shakespeare. In one of his most penetrating articles, *A Plague on Both Your Houses,* he analysed the power struggle between two erstwhile comrades of the People's Action Party. He contributed articles, often writing under various pen names, including Hwang Toe Chin and Wong Tjilik. The consummate journalist, he would stay up all night to write his articles, downing many cups of black coffee. The *Sunday Mail* was the weekly forum for debating topical issues and Wong comments from the savants of the two universities, politicians, trade unionists and student activists. Wong published articles by intellectuals from both sides of the Cold War, the USA and the USSR.

Francis Wong was also the founding Editor of the short-lived *Singapore Herald,* a tabloid newspaper in Singapore whose publishing licence was suspended by the Singapore government in May 1971. The paper was accused of being funded by questionable foreign sources and working up agitation against national policies and institutions. According to him, it was a most painful exit from his first love, journalism. In his second career, he was the man behind the Parkway Parade project, one of the largest shopping complexes in the 1980s.

Francis Wong was a dedicated newspaper journalist, genuinely passionate and concerned about the issue of press freedom.

Pioneer in Bioengineering and Nanotechnology

Jackie Yi-Ru Ying

Jackie Yi-Ru Ying has been named as one of 100 young people in the world expected to be leading 21st century innovators. At thirty-four, she became the youngest professor at the Massachusetts Institute of Technology. She has the honour of heading the newly-established Institute of Bioengineering and Nanotechnology as its Executive Director. Although an American citizen, she considers Singapore her home.

Ying was born in Taiwan and came to Singapore at the age of one. She lived in Singapore, from 1973–1981, when her father was the senior lecturer in Chinese Literature in the then Nanyang University. She received her primary and secondary education at Raffles Girls' School.

"I have very strong emotional ties with this country and I grew up here. It was the best part of my life and I very much wanted to come back." She has many happy memories of her childhood and teenage years. "In fact, I didn't want to go to the US. I remember fighting with my father. All my friends were here." When she was fifteen, her father uprooted the family of five and moved to New York, partly because permanent residence status was hard to come by in those days.

Ying obtained her doctorate at Princeton University in 1991 and joined the Chemical Engineering faculty of MIT and was appointed a full Professor in 2001, the youngest to do so. With her brilliant record, she won academic fellowships every year and sits on the editorial board of many scientific journals in her field.

She was headhunted by the Agency for Science Technology and Research (A*STAR) to be the Chief Executive of Singapore's Institute of Bioengineering and Nanotechnology (IBN). Her immediate task was to develop a pool of scientists and commercialise the Institute's discoveries. Her work involves developing a new generation of biomaterials, processes and devices which will help the biotech industry to be on par with the intense global competition. "It allows me to do fundamental research and train the students on entrepreneurship."

Despite the hype surrounding her research as a potential money-spinner, Ying is realistic. "A lot of the work we do is at the cutting edge and nobody else has the knowledge to take over. We have to train people from the start. At MIT, I produced two to four students a year. Here, our aim is 60 students and post-doctoral fellows a year. Research quality will be crucial in the longer term. It's critical to have credibility to attract business." The 41-year-old professor has ambitious plans for the pioneering facilities which will have 250 staff in three years. She has dug into her wide contact base and intends to recruit top-notch researchers into the Institute.

Ying was featured in the MIT's centennial issue as one of the world's 100 young people expected to lead the 21st century innovators. An authority on nanomaterials — tiny materials that can be used to produce a wide range of products — she works more than 70 hours weekly.

This remarkable woman is confident that Singapore has the potential to be a leading Biomedical Science hub. Her advice to young scientists is that they should gain as much hands-on experience as possible and conduct research with leading scientists. It is essential to be able to think outside the box in order to come up with novel inventions.

Dim Sum Dolly

Emma Yong

Emma Yong is a pioneering actress of the emerging Singapore theatre. She turned down a promising international career to keep company with other home-grown talents. Her ambition was to be a writer. She won the Angus Ross Award for topping the International Advanced Level for English from among 7,000 international candidates.

Emma Yong studied at Nanyang Primary, Raffles Girls' School (1988–1991) and Raffles Junior College (1992–1993). She graduated in English from University College, London, and holds a Post-Graduate Diploma from the Mount View Academy of Theatre Arts.

"My happiest memories of RGS are of my times spent in the choir. We had so much fun learning how to sing from the wonderful Welsh teacher. I really enjoyed performing in the annual school musical. Being an all-girls' school, we had to play the male parts too. The hardest part of being a prefect was having to book your school mates if their skirts were too short. But I was also given so many opportunities to learn about leadership and taking responsibility." She attributes her success in winning the 1993 International Advanced Level English Literature prize to her inspiring teacher and to her term as president of the Film Club of RJC, which made her more sensitive in her writing. "I love literature, so I thought I would become a writer."

For the six-year-old Emma, her first encounter with the Arts was to accompany her elder sister to her ballet class. While at RJC, Emma was initiated into her first musical *Bugis Street.* She continued acting when she was in the university. "It was then that I realised how vital theatre was to me. I knew that it was the only thing that could get me out of bed and eager to go to work. Nothing inspired the same enthusiasm." It heralded the start of a glittering career in television and on stage, through which she has captivated audiences with her acting and singing for the past ten years. *Dim Sum Dollies, Ah Kong's Birthday Party, Cabaret* and *Boeing Boeing* are among her notable performances.

"One of my favourites will always be *Mail Order Brides.* It was immensely difficult to do. The subject matter drained us emotionally. The best experience in theatre tends to revolve around the people you work with. I always appreciate the fact the people in this industry are such passionate, loving, warm people. The downside of theatre is dealing with the broken promises and shattered dreams." For Emma, a *geisha,* a mail order China bride or a cabaret girl, life is an endless stage. She did not launch her career in London because she did not relish being cast in stereotypically racial roles. She was also homesick and missed the local food.

Books, music and movies are essential for her artistic mind. "I go for books which are emotional and deep. I like black humour. As an artist, it is important to open your mind to as many art forms as possible. Broadway music always tells a story. Every lyric drives the plot forward. It is never about meaningless words and easy listening melodies."

For Emma, satisfaction comes from becoming the character she is playing and creating truth on stage. "I don't see myself as having arrived or attaining a big achievement. It has been many small steps over ten years." At the age of 30, the mezzo-soprano crowned her illustrious career with her solo concert *From Bjork to Broadway* at the Esplanade.

Away from the public spotlight, how does she see herself? "I'm actually quite an intense person. My friends complain that we always have to talk about life, death, love and relationships. I'm also serious when it comes to my work. I don't want to be complacent. So I tend to be a bit of a perfectionist." Does she have an inspiring message for budding actors and actresses? "If you put action into what you want to do and you are willing to work hard, there's nothing to stop you from achieving your dream."

In Emma and others like her, Singapore's emerging theatre scene is assured of a promising and bright future.

High Flying Entrepreneur

Diana Young

Diana Young was a very successful woman entrepreneur. She was the Chief Executive of her aerospace firm and the first woman President of the Association of Small and Medium Enterprises. Aviation was in her blood and her ambition was to be a pilot. An intrepid jet-setter, she was tragically killed in a car accident in Xi'an in Central China in 2004.

Young was born in 1957. She studied at Margaret Drive Primary School, Tanglin Secondary School and RGS, where she completed her 'A' levels. She was also a formidable debater and prefect. A promising student, she was the teacher's pet. During the school holidays, she sold hamburgers at football matches in the National Stadium and also gave private tuition. Already a budding entrepreneur, the young Diana earned her own pocket money. She was very determined and strong-headed. She had a black belt in taekwondo.

Diana was the sixth of seven children. Her family lived in an *attap* house in Alexandra Road. In the book, *Candle Burning Bright* dedicated to Diana's memory, her sister Ivy writes, "As a child, Diana stood out. She was also born a beauty. From young, she was given the nickname of 'Big Eye Chick' because she had the biggest and brightest pair of eyes with long black eyelashes. She was also the fairest and smartest." She was fascinated by planes and joined the Junior Flying Club. But that ambition was dashed as she had colour blindness.

Diana worked in various occupations — as a real estate agent, secretary, administrator and trader. When her business did not take off, she ventured to North America and the Philippines in search of gold.

Diana's initiation into the aviation industry began when she was managing two Malaysian companies. She rebuilt a fleet of grounded aeroplanes and made them fly again. However, she was not content to rest on her laurels as a successful Corporate Manager. Her indomitable spirit and entrepreneurial vision drove her to her bold decision to be her own boss. She founded Mil-Com Aerospace in 1994, with its acronym to incorporate its Military and Commercial operations. Mil-Com started as a distributor of aircraft components in Asia. It expanded its operations to offer aerospace support services, retrofitting and maintenance of commercial aircraft. She developed a niche market for her company in Singapore and the region. She also set up her own aerospace training centre, which was aimed to provide aircraft technical training to aviation personnel in Singapore, Asia and beyond. Its strategic partner was Alteon-Boeing.

Diana Young was named 'Woman of the Year' for 2002. Her company also won the 'Enterprise 51' and Quality Class awards. She was the first Woman President of the Association of Small and Medium Enterprises and was their inspiring mentor. "Seize the day. A day that goes by will never come back again. Know every aspect of your own business and industry. Have a positive mental attitude to meet the challenges facing the company. Understand and know that money is the lifeblood of business." She always believed in the importance of customer service and in the personal touch.

She also trained her two teenage children, so that they could learn about the business early. Sometimes they accompanied her on her trips. "My son carries my suitcases and my daughter acts as my secretary."

Her colleagues said that she boarded planes with the regularity which other people did for taxis. But Diana Young was not spoilt by her success and had her feet planted firmly on the ground. She was never carried away by her brilliant rise to success. She was modest about her achievements. "Being in the aviation business, I'm usually in the hotels closest to the airport. I fly Business Class and sometimes, Economy. First Class is for people with blue blood and who don't have to work. I don't like to sit in the priority passenger lounge. I prefer the common waiting area where I can watch people and assess their behaviour. When I see unpleasant behaviour, I tell myself not to do the same."

Diana Young died in 2004 in a car accident, while on a business trip to Xi'an in Central China. She was forty-eight. Singapore had lost a very successful and dynamic woman entrepreneur.

Straddling Two Cultures

Yu Chun Yee

For Yu Chun Yee, going from the Chinese High School to Raffles Institution was a culture shock. Chinese High was the breeding ground for aspiring revolutionaries, drawing inspiration from an emerging China. RI was the cradle of the privileged English-educated elite who celebrated Empire Day with the song *Land of Hope and Glory* and were the beneficiaries of British colonial rule. But the young Yu was impressed by neither — he only wanted to be a concert pianist.

Yu was born in Shanghai and came to Singapore at the age of one. His parents had fled from China in the wake of the Sino-Japanese War. He did not take the conventional route to RI. It all started in 1954, when he was awarded a scholarship to study at the Royal College of Music. The colonials in the Education Department felt that he should be better acquainted with the English language and culture. RI was the natural choice. Nevertheless, Yu had to sit for an examination in Maths, English and Science, which he passed with flying colours.

His father was the Chief Editor of the Chinese newspaper *Nanyang Siang Pao*. Yu learned to play the piano at a very early age. He was launched into his career when he won a competition in 1954. It was the first ever competition organised by the Singapore Music Society and was open to all, including foreigners. The adjudicator was the world-renowned Julius Katchen. He was so impressed by Yu's performance that he gave a charity concert to raise funds for his scholarship. However, Yu's hopes were nearly dashed when certain quarters claimed that his win was a fluke. So Yu had to compete again the following year. He confounded his critics by winning again.

Yu's first days in RI were for him nothing short of a culture shock. It was the first time that he came into contact with Malay and Indian boys. He was bewildered by cricket, rugby and hockey, although he had represented Chinese High in table tennis and basketball. "Chinese High and RI had diametrically opposite philosophies of education. The former stressed the holistic and total development of education. As for the latter, it was compartmentalised into subjects, like Arts and Science. Chinese school students are generally better in Mathematics and Science, because they learned by rote."

More culture shock followed, when he arrived in London. But Yu persisted, determined to succeed. At the Royal College of Music, he thrived in competition with other outstanding students. On graduating, he was offered a scholarship which took him to France and Italy. He became Professor of Piano at the age of 35 and he held the post for 30 years. For his contributions to music, Queen Elizabeth II the Queen Mother, conferred Yu the FRCM — the 1st Asian to receive this honour. On returning to Singapore, Yu has taught some of the pianists who have achieved international fame. He was Vice-President of NAFA prior to his retirement and started the School of Young Talents.

Yu is buoyant about Singapore's current Arts scene. It was not so long ago that Singapore was written off as a 'cultural desert'. However, he laments that our best musicians are not given recognition for their talents. "It is still very tough for them to earn a living as professionals."

Yu recalls that when he was awarded his scholarship, his father's friend had asked his father, "Do you really want your son to be a cultural beggar?" Nevertheless, he is cautiously optimistic. "What is needed is a fundamental change in the public perception of the artist as the poorer relative of the scientist. The artist can also be our goodwill ambassador, displaying Singapore's rich cultural heritage and talents to our neighbours and to the world."

Photo Credits

We are grateful to the following for permission to reproduce the photographs and images in this book:

SPH – The Straits Times
for Michael Chan Chew Koon, Goh Choo San, Siow Lee Chin, Margaret Leng Tan, Teng Pei Wah (or Tang Pui Wah) and Francis Wong Tze Kan.

The Collection of the Ministry of Information, Communications and the Arts, Courtesy of National Archives of Singapore
for Edmund William Barker, Goh Chok Tong, Yusof Ishak, S. Jayakumar, Lee Kuan Yew, Lim Bo Seng, Lim Hng Kiang, Lim Yew Hock, David Marshall, George Oehlers, Judith Prakash, S. Rajaratnam, Abdullah Tarmugi, Tee Tua Ba and Wee Kim Wee.

The Collection of Benjamin Sheares, Courtesy of National Archives of Singapore
for Benjamin Sheares.

National Archives of Singapore
for Tan Cheng Lock.

The Collection of Raffles College, Courtesy of National Archives of Singapore
for Lee Siow Mong.

Dr Nicholas Aplin, Physical Education and Sports Science, NIE
for Tan Eng Yoon.

Raffles Girls' School (Secondary)
for Mae Noleen Oehlers.

As well as to those profiled in this book, family members, friends and colleagues, who generously came forward with these invaluable photos.

Disclaimer